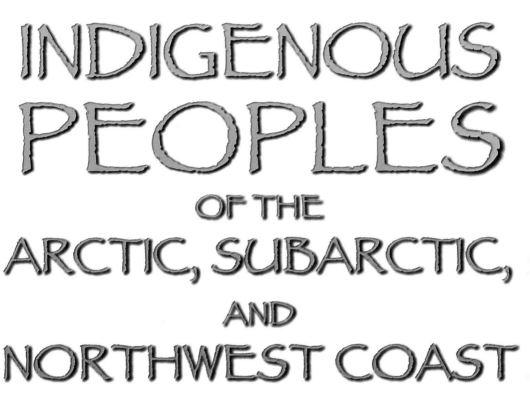

INDIGENOUS PEOPLES

OF THE
ARCTIC, SUBARCTIC,
AND
NORTHWEST COAST

NATIVE AMERICAN TRIBES

INDIGENOUS PEOPLES

OF THE ARCTIC, SUBARCTIC, AND NORTHWEST COAST

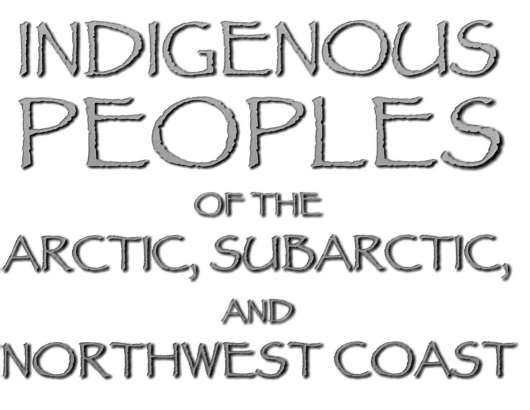

EDITED BY KATHLEEN KUIPER, MANAGER, ARTS AND CULTURE

Britannica
Educational Publishing

IN ASSOCIATION WITH

ROSEN
EDUCATIONAL SERVICES

Published in 2012 by Britannica Educational Publishing
(a trademark of Encyclopædia Britannica, Inc.)
in association with Rosen Educational Services, LLC
29 East 21st Street, New York, NY 10010.

First Edition

Britannica Educational Publishing
Michael I. Levy: Executive Editor
J.E. Luebering: Senior Manager
Marilyn L. Barton: Senior Coordinator, Production Control
Steven Bosco: Director, Editorial Technologies
Lisa S. Braucher: Senior Producer and Data Editor
Yvette Charboneau: Senior Copy Editor
Kathy Nakamura: Manager, Media Acquisition
Kathleen Kuiper: Manager, Arts and Culture

Rosen Educational Services
Heather M. Moore Niver: Editor
Nelson Sá: Art Director
Cindy Reiman: Photography Manager
Karen Huang: Photo Researcher
Matthew Cauli: Designer, Cover Design
Introduction by Kathleen Kuiper

Library of Congress Cataloging-in-Publication Data

Indigenous peoples of the Arctic, Subarctic, and Northwest Coast / edited by Kathleen Kuiper.
    p. cm. — (Native American tribes)
"In association with Britannica Educational Publishing, Rosen Educational Services."
Includes bibliographical references and index.
ISBN 978-1-61530-658-9 (library binding)
1. Indians of North America — Northwest Coast of North Americ — History. 2. Indians of
North America — Northwest Coast of North America — Social life and customs. 3. Inuit —
Greenland — History. 4. Inuit — Greenland — Social life and customs. I. Kuiper, Kathleen.
E78.N78A44 2012
979.004'97 — dc22

                                                                                2011013487

Manufactured in the United States of America

On the cover: An Inupiat hunter in Alaska. *Rex Ziak/Stone/Getty Images*

On pages x-xi: A dogsled rushes across the snows of Iqaluit, Nunavut, Canada. *AFP/ Getty Images*

On pages 1, 21, 39, 57, 77, 102, 121, 124, 127: Aurora borealis, Gilbert Plains, Manitoba, Canada. *Shutterstock.com*

CONTENTS

INTRODUCTION

S now, miles of it, reaching to the horizon and 360 degrees around you, as far as you can see. There's not much in the way of landmarks to help you see where you've been or where you're going. If the sun is out, you need extra eye protection to avoid snow blindness. And if the sun isn't out, you might be in trouble, too. A blizzard can blow up without warning.

When you're hungry, there are few choices for food. If the hunters have been lucky, there's meat, but little by way of vegetables. (Some people might consider that a plus.) You're pretty much at the mercy of hunters and family tailors for clothes—which are always recommended—and there are not many alternative outfits.

Just imagine what it would be like to live in the Arctic. If you'd like a visual example, take a look at Akira Kurosawa's film, *Derzu Usala*, from 1975. Although it's set in the Siberian Arctic rather than the American North, it gives not only a great sense of the challenges of life in the Arctic, but also some idea of the beliefs and practices of the area's aboriginal peoples.

But perhaps the most authentic story can be found in *Atanarjuat (The Fast Runner)*, filmed in Nunavut, Canada, with an Inuit director, actors, and film crew. This 2001 film offers a wealth of information about the material and social culture of the Inuit. It gives a clear idea of who would choose to stay in such a brutal, terrifyingly gorgeous region. And why.

Like that movie in its poetic way, this book answers those questions and more. It examines the history, ways of life, and economic strategies of the peoples of the North American Arctic, as well as those of the Subarctic and the coastal Pacific Northwest.

For the most part, Arctic peoples live beyond the climatic limits of agriculture, drawing subsistence from hunting, trapping, and fishing or from herding. Thus changes in climate, rather than simple latitude, determine the effective boundaries of the circumpolar region, and these climatic gradients have their counterparts in the major environmental transitions. Of these transitions, the most important is the tree line, which marks the northern margin of the coniferous forest, or taiga. Between this limit and the coasts of the Arctic Ocean, the land consists of open tundra, though in regions of high altitude, pockets of tundra lie enclosed within the forest zone.

Among more southern people, Arctic environments are commonly thought to be barren and inhospitable, habitable only by virtue of the extreme physical endurance and technical virtuosity of the peoples who dwell in them. Though they do, without a doubt, possess these qualities, this view of the far north rests on a misconception. The image of the remote wilderness, to be conquered through a struggle for survival, belongs to the language of the alien explorer, not to that of the native. For indigenous people, the circumpolar environment is neither hostile nor forbidding but familiar and generous, offering the gift of livelihood to those who treat it with consideration and respect.

Seasons of scarcity certainly occur, but these alternate with periods of extraordinary abundance. The continuous daylight of the warm Arctic summer, coupled with ample surface water from melting snow, allows for a phenomenal rate of growth of surface vegetation, and this in turn attracts a multitude of animals, many of them of migratory species. Warm ocean currents around some Arctic coasts are likewise conducive to an abundance of marine fauna. It is not, then, scarcity that characterizes the Arctic environment but rather its seasonality. The resources available for human subsistence—which are primarily faunal rather than vegetable—tend to occur in great concentrations at particular times of year, rather than being widely dispersed and continuously available. These fluctuations naturally affect the settlement patterns and movements of human populations, as do the marked seasonal variations in the length of day and night and in the opportunities afforded by the landscape for transport and travel.

The three major environmental zones of forest, tundra, and coast, and the transitions between them, establish the range of conditions to which the ways of life of the Arctic peoples are adapted. Broadly speaking, there are four basic kinds of adaptation. The first is entirely confined within the forest and is based on the exploitation of its fairly diverse resources of land animals, birds, and fish. Local groups tend to be small and widely scattered, each exploiting a range of territory around a fixed, central location. The second kind of adaptation spans the transition between forest and tundra. It is characterized by a heavy, year-round dependence on herds of caribou, whose annual migrations from the forest to the tundra in spring and from the tundra back to the forest in autumn are matched by the lengthy nomadic movements of the associated human groups; in North America these are hunters who aim to intercept the herds on their migrations. The third kind of adaptation, most common among Inuit groups, involves a seasonal movement in the reverse direction, between the hunting of sea mammals on the coast in winter and spring and the hunting of caribou and fishing on the inland tundra in summer and autumn. Fourth, typical of cultures of the northern Pacific coast is an exclusively maritime adaptation. People live year-round in relatively large, coastal settlements, hunting the rich resources of marine mammals from boats in summer and from the ice in winter.

In northern North America only Indian peoples practice the forest and forest-tundra modes of subsistence. Coastal and coastal-tundra adaptations are the exclusive preserve of the Inuit and of the Aleut of the northern Pacific islands.

Indian cultures are thus essentially tied to the forest, whereas Inuit and Aleut cultures are entirely independent of the forest and tied rather to the coast. Conventionally, this contrast has been taken to mark the distinction between peoples of the Subarctic and those of the Arctic. Thus the indigenous peoples of northernmost North America, the Eskimo (Inuit and Yupik) and Aleut, are considered under the Arctic label, whereas the Indian groups are dealt with separately in the chapters on American Subarctic people.

Perhaps it would be useful at this point to discuss the terminology used to refer to the aboriginal peoples of the North American continent. In the past 500 years, indigenous Americans have been called American Indian, Native American, First Nation, Eskimo, Inuit, and Native Alaskan. Some of these terms are used almost interchangeably, while others indicate relatively specific entities.

The term "American Indian" is often used to refer to the indigenous cultures of the Western Hemisphere in general. Its constituent parts were in use from at least the early 16th century. The word "Indian" came to be used because Christopher Columbus repeatedly expressed the mistaken belief that he had reached the shores of South Asia. Convinced he was correct, Columbus fostered the use of the term "Indios" (originally, "person from the Indus valley") to refer to the peoples of the so-called New World. The term "America" came into use as a referent to the continents of the Western Hemisphere as early as 1507, when the German cartographer Martin Waldseemüller published a map naming the continents of the Western Hemisphere for the Italian explorer Amerigo Vespucci. The word "American" was soon thereafter appended to "Indian" to differentiate the indigenous peoples of these regions from those of South Asia.

In the 1960s many activists in the United States and Canada rejected the name American Indian because it was seen as a misnomer and sometimes carried racist connotations. In these countries "Native American" soon became the preferred term of reference, although many (and perhaps most) indigenous individuals living north of the Rio Grande continued to refer to themselves as Indians.

Europeans initially called the peoples of the American Arctic Eskimo, a term meaning "eaters of raw flesh" in the languages of the neighbouring Abenaki and Ojibwa nations. Finding that referent inappropriate, American Arctic peoples initiated the use of their self-names during the 1960s. Those of southern and western Alaska became known as the Yupik, while those of northern and eastern Alaska and all of Canada became known as the Inuit. The 1960s were also a period during which Alaska's aboriginal peoples initiated a variety of land claims. As an expression of unity, these diverse societies, which included not only the Yupik and Inuit but also nations such as the Aleut, Gwich'in, Deg Xinag, and Tanaina, adopted the umbrella term "Native Alaskan."

In the 1970s Native Americans in Canada began to use the term "First Nation" as their preferred self-name. The Canadian government adopted this use but did not furnish a legal definition for it. The Métis and Inuit preferred not to be called First Nations, and thus Canadians especially use the terms "aboriginal peoples" or "aboriginal" nations when referring to the Inuit, Métis, and First Nations peoples of Canada in aggregate.

By the end of the 20th century, native peoples from around the world had begun to encourage others to use tribal self-names when possible (i.e., to refer to an individual as a Hopi, Xavante, or Sami) and the word "indigenous" when a descriptor for their shared political identity was more suitable. This preference was recognized by the United Nations when it established the Permanent Forum on Indigenous Issues (2000) and passed the Declaration of the Rights of Indigenous Peoples (2007). In the United States, however, many individuals of indigenous heritage continued to refer to aboriginal Americans, in aggregate, as Indians. In this context, it's worthwhile to reflect on the importance of names. They reveal much about our attitudes toward others and ourselves.

The second cultural area discussed in this book is that of American Subarctic peoples. This region is located north of the humid continental climate, from about 50° to 70° N, in a broad swath extending from Alaska to Newfoundland in North America. The land consists chiefly of taiga, or boreal forest, a moist and marshy geographic area dominated by conifers—such as spruce and fir—that begins where the tundra ends. Winter there is a long, bitterly cold period with short, clear days, relatively little precipitation (mostly in the form of snow), and low humidity.

Subarctic peoples traditionally used a variety of technologies to cope with the cold northern winters and were adept in the production of well-insulated homes, fur garments, toboggans, ice chisels, and snowshoes. The traditional diet included game animals such as moose, caribou, bison (in the southern locales), beaver, and fish, as well as wild plant foods such as berries, roots, and sap. Food resources were distributed quite thinly over the subarctic landscape, and starvation was always a potential problem.

The fading of this way of life is the subject of Joseph Boyden's powerful 2005 novel, *Three Day Road*. It examines changes in the lives of two Cree men. Not for the faint-hearted, it is about many things—the horrors of World War I and the ravages of drug use—but it is also about the worldview of the Cree, the power of the spirit called windigo, and the effects of nonnative people on Cree lives.

The third culture area discussed in this volume is that of the Northwest Coast, a narrow belt of Pacific coastland and offshore islands from the southern border of Alaska to northwestern California. Although the sea and various mountain ranges provide the region with distinct boundaries to the east, north, and west, the transition from the Northwest Coast to the California culture area is gradual, and some scholars may discuss some of the southernmost groups included here with the California Indians.

This area is warmed by the Kuroshio (a Japanese word meaning "Black Current"), a surface Pacific Ocean current that is so-called because it appears a deeper blue than does the sea through which it flows. This current moderates land temperatures—which are rarely hot and seldom drop below freezing—and deluges the region with rain. Because of this climate, the peoples of the Northwest Coast lacked little.

The peoples of the Northwest Coast had abundant and reliable supplies of salmon and other fish, sea mammals, shellfish, birds, and a variety of wild food plants. Their resources were so rich that these peoples are unique among nonagricultural groups in having created highly stratified societies of hereditary elites, commoners, and slaves.

Most groups built villages near waterways or the coast. Each village also had rights to an upland territory from which the residents could obtain terrestrial foods. Dwellings were rectilinear structures built of timbers or planks and were usually quite large, as the members of a corporate "house" typically lived together in one building. Northwest Coast cultures are known for their fine wood and stone carvings, large and seaworthy watercraft, memorial or totem poles, and basketry. They are also known for the potlatch, a feast associated with the bestowal of lavish gifts.

To sum up, then, this book discusses three culture areas: the Arctic, Subarctic, and Northwest Coast. We hope that, beyond the historical and cultural information it provides, it prompts you to ponder many things: human strategies for survival, exploration, conquest, and above all, mindfulness of our planet and our fellow travelers and the other creatures with whom we share it.

The treeless shores and tundra-covered coastal hinterlands of northernmost North America and Greenland are inhabited by Eskimo (Inuit and Yupik/ Yupiit) and Aleuts. Canadian and Greenlandic Arctic peoples are generally called Inuit. The U.S. peoples of this region may be known as Eskimos and Aleuts or Native Alaskans. Because of their close social, genetic, and linguistic relations to Yupik speakers in Alaska, the Yupik-speaking peoples living near the Bering Sea in Siberia are sometimes discussed with these groups. (Scholarly custom separates the American Arctic peoples from other American Indians, from whom they are distinguished by various linguistic, physiological, and cultural differences.)

HISTORY OF SETTLEMENT

In northernmost North America, only mainland Alaska and a small northwestern corner of Canada remained largely unglaciated during the latest ice age of the Pleistocene (about 2,600,000 to 11,700 years ago). These areas were joined to northeastern Asia—also largely without ice—across land exposed by low sea levels at what is now the Bering Strait. To the east and south, the way into the North American continent was blocked with ice and unnegotiable terrain from about 25,000 to 11,000 BCE.

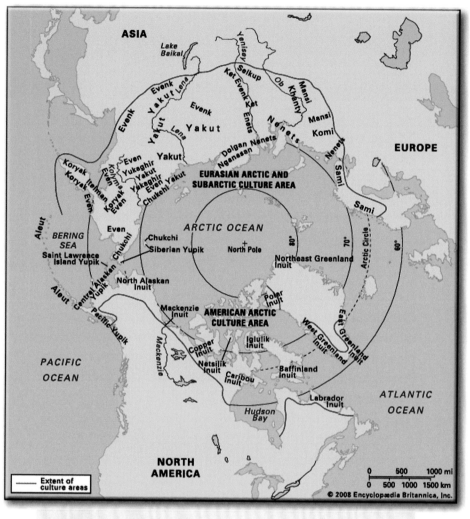

Distribution of Arctic peoples.

PALEO-ARCTIC AND PALEO-INDIAN TRADITIONS

The earliest residents of the American Arctic are known from this area of ice-free Alaska and northwest Canada. They arrived as early as perhaps 12,000 BCE and can be referred to as members of the Paleo-Arctic cultural tradition. They made cutting implements in a style common to northeast Asia that was characterized by slender flakes struck from specially prepared stone cores—flakes referred to by archaeologists as "blades," many of them small (less than 5 cm [2 in] in length) and classed as "microblades." Some blades were apparently set into the edges of bone or antler batons, thus forming knives or projectile heads. With the latter, the Paleo-Arctic people hunted terrestrial animals. Caribou appear to have been their preferred food, although they also hunted elk, forms of bison now extinct (e.g., *Bison antiquus*), and perhaps mammoths. Blade and microblade tools had appeared earlier on the Asian side of the North Pacific, notably in Siberia and portions of the Japanese islands. Evidence from those regions also suggests a reliance on terrestrial, rather than coastal, resources.

In approximately 11,000 BCE, as thawing ice caps began to open access to the rest of North America and flood the land bridge to Asia, a change occurred in sites in north Alaska: the production of microblades decreased, while small projectile points or knife blades of stone, more fully shaped by chipping than were the microblades, appeared. Some archaeologists have attempted without appreciable success to find the beginning of this change in northeast Siberia. Others have suggested that it represents a development within the early Paleo-Arctic tradition itself or that it is in fact a reflection of people already in the American heartland to the southeast, although the time and manner of their arrival there remains unknown at this time. In any event, by 10,000 BCE there was a resurgence of the microblade-producing sites of the Paleo-Arctic tradition. In northern Alaska at the same time there also appeared stone spear points that bear a striking resemblance to the artifacts known from the same period in other parts of North America.

Like its southern counterparts, this material culture and its makers are referred to as Paleo-Indian. Most archaeologists presume the Arctic Paleo-Indians were a new influx of people who moved north from regions to the southeast, probably following (and hunting) herds of bison and other animals as they expanded into the areas where the ice had retreated. That they were in some way descended from people present in Alaska in that earlier interval when microblades were uncommon seems possible but is yet to be demonstrated. The sites used by the Paleo-Arctic (microblade) and Paleo-Indian (spear-point) cultures are in somewhat different areas, and so these groups are thought to have been distinct peoples.

By at least 8000 BCE the presence of Paleo-Arctic people can be recognized on the Alaska Peninsula in southern mainland Alaska. At almost exactly the same moment, their characteristic microblade tools appear in a few sites on the coast in southeastern Alaska and British Columbia, suggesting a movement of Paleo-Arctic descendants south. When microblades appear on the central coast of British Columbia, they are found at sites that include distinctively different artifacts. This seems to indicate that the Paleo-Arctic people met with others who were already living in the area. Although food remains from this period are seldom preserved, evidence indicates that the transition from a terrestrial subsistence economy to one based on oceanside resources was complete within a millennium.

Beginning about 7000 BCE, sites with blades and microblades appear in the eastern Aleutian Islands. Although food remains are lacking in these sites, it is clear that the occupants lived on ocean resources, as there are no other resources present in any significant quantity. Notably, all these Paleo-Arctic–related appearances on the coast (of both islands and mainland) occur south of the regions in which coastlines freeze fast during the winter.

The end of the Paleo-Arctic tradition occurred about 5500 BCE. Certainly, by 5000 BCE the signs of remnant

Paleo-Arctic–related people had been eclipsed both in the interior and on the southern coast. In the interior, new styles of artifacts constitute the Northern Archaic tradition. In general, Northern Archaic sites are located within what were the expanding northern forests. Although some Northern Archaic people left traces outside the forest limits, they generally avoided the coasts. Their artifacts include fairly large chipped-stone points with stems or notches near the points' base (stemming and notching both facilitate hafting a point to its shaft). Northern Archaic food resources were terrestrial. If the sequence of major tool types in the American Arctic is analogous to that represented to the south, this tradition may have developed from the earlier Paleo-Indian culture of the north, although direct evidence for this has thus far not been presented.

OCEAN BAY TRADITION

By 5000 BCE, changes are also seen at sites along parts of the northernmost Pacific coast, including the eastern Aleutians, where the sea remains open in winter. These sites are characterized by new kinds of artifacts, notably large stone projectile points, stone basins for burning sea-mammal oil, and harpoon heads of bone. When combined with evidence from food remains, these materials clearly indicate that local residents relied heavily upon marine mammals, including those that required the use of boats well offshore. Scholars have not reached consensus on a name for the people represented by this new material culture, but some have referred to them as members of the Ocean Bay tradition.

Up to about 4000 BCE, this tradition was common to the residents of the Kodiak region and the Aleutian Islands. Shortly thereafter, however, these two groups began to develop in different directions. People in the Aleutians carried aspects of Ocean Bay technology with them as they moved farther and farther west through the chain of islands, arriving at the most distant islands, Agattu and Attu, not later than about 600 BCE. On the Pacific coast around Kodiak, however, the people began to fashion stone artifacts by grinding, a technology that persisted throughout later millennia and was markedly different from that used in the Aleutians.

SMALL TOOL TRADITION

The first residents of the winter-freezing coasts of the north appeared only after 3000 BCE, when people of the Arctic Small Tool tradition began to replace any Northern Archaic people who were exploiting the largely treeless lands immediately inland from the coasts. Predominantly terrestrial in subsistence orientation—hunting especially caribou and musk ox and taking river and lake fish—the people of the Arctic Small Tool tradition also exploited coastal resources on a seasonal basis. These people are thought to have been new immigrants from Neolithic northeast Asia, as their material culture is characterized by diminutive stone artifacts similar to those found in that region, albeit without the pottery that is usually found on Asian sites.

Although leaving evidence of neither sleds nor boats, by 2500 BCE the descendants of the Small Tool people had exploded across the Arctic Archipelago of Canada to northernmost Greenland, in some areas turning more and more to coastal resources. At about the same time, they also expanded within Alaska south to the Alaska Peninsula, where their southern limit coincided with that of heavy winter coastal drift ice and intruded in some limited areas to the North Pacific itself near Cook Inlet. Within a few centuries they moved also into the tundra-covered Barren Grounds west of Hudson Bay, displacing earlier peoples who had exploited Barren Grounds caribou. Along the

Musk oxen were often hunted by people of the Arctic Small Tool tradition. Hemera Technologies/Photos.com/Thinkstock

northeastern coast of the continent, they penetrated southward as far as the Gulf of St. Lawrence, again to the southern edge of heavy winter sea ice.

In northern Canada and Greenland the Small Tool folk gradually developed into those of the Dorset culture, who by 800 BCE had created techniques for hunting seals through their breathing holes in winter sea ice and developed substantial dwellings of sod and rocks that they heated with lamps of sea-mammal oil. In some areas the Dorset culture is thought to have persisted until about 1300 CE.

In Alaska the material culture of the Small Tool people was replaced by that of the Norton culture in approximately 500 BCE. These people made pottery similar to that found in contemporary Siberia, and their substantial villages of semisubterranean houses appeared along the coast from the Bering Sea to the Beaufort Sea, near the present northern border of Alaska with Canada.

DORSET CULTURE

The prehistoric culture of Greenland and the Canadian eastern Arctic as far south as present-day Newfoundland is called the Dorset culture (or, in Greenlandic, Kalaallit Nunaat). It existed from approximately 800 BCE to 1300 CE. Its English-language name comes from excavations made at Cape Dorset at Baffin Island.

Several theories about the origin of Dorset culture have been posited: that it originated in Alaska or another part of the western Arctic, that it derived from or was strongly influenced by certain Archaic or Woodland cultures farther south, or that it was a fundamentally Eskimo (Inuit) culture that developed in place in the Canadian eastern Arctic from a culture called Pre-Dorset, with little external influence.

For subsistence, Dorset people depended primarily on sea mammals such as seals and walrus. They also fished and hunted land mammals and birds as the opportunity arose. At the time, dogs and dogsleds were unknown, so the people used small hand sleds to transport bulky materials. The bow-drill, a common Inuit tool, was not part of the Dorset tool kit. Dorset harpoon heads and foreshafts, knives, lamps, and chipped-stone implements were distinctive. Ornaments were made of bone, ivory, or wood, and occasionally engraved. Small ivory or bone animal and human figures, which were sometimes naturalistic and sometimes stylized or grotesque, may have been used as amulets or as a form of hunting magic.

Dorset settlements were located on coasts and generally consisted of semisubterranean houses and large meetinghouses. Skin-covered tents were probably used during the summer. Evidence suggests that the Dorset people were seasonal nomads who traveled in small groups.

It is not certain when Dorset culture disappeared, but it was after members of the Thule culture arrived from Alaska, for there are indications of contact between the two groups. Climatic changes, notably the onset of the Medieval Cool Period—a period of increased cold that occurred in the Northern Hemisphere from approximately 1250–1500 CE—may have contributed to the decline of Dorset culture. The extent to which the Dorset people influenced the later indigenous cultures of Canada and Greenland is unclear. Some later types of tools clearly derived from this culture, and a group of Inuit who survived in the area until 1903 may have been direct descendants of the Dorset people.

Norton people hunted sea mammals in open water—some of their harpoons were large enough for whaling—as well as interior animals, including caribou. They also took lake and river fish. On much of the Alaska mainland, people of the Norton tradition endured until the end of the 1st millennium CE, a period when other major developments were taking place in the islands and on the Asian coast near the Bering Strait.

THULE CULTURE

In the area around the strait, an increasing ability to hunt in the open sea led to the development of the Northern Maritime, or Thule, cultural tradition. In this area the tradition is recognizable by 200 CE and in some cases perhaps a century or two earlier. It is characterized by ground slate tools, ivory harpoon heads (often decoratively engraved), lamps made of clay or mud, and a heavy reliance on sea mammals. By c. 700 CE, the ancestral Thule people (or their culture) had expanded into Alaska north of the Bering Strait, where by 900–1000 CE the mature Thule culture, or Thule proper, appeared.

Thule culture proved to be the most adaptable of the Arctic, expanding rapidly to the coasts of Alaska, the eastern Chukchi Peninsula of Asia, and up the rivers of the Alaska mainland. This culture's use of the large open skin boat, or umiak, for walrus and whale hunting, the kayak for sealing, and the dogsled for winter land transportation enabled the people to increase their subsistence options and geographic range. After 1000 CE, perhaps moving in pursuit of whales (whose locations were shifting because of changing ice conditions), they moved rapidly across northernmost Canada to Greenland. In these areas, they established new settlements of stone and sod houses at key locations while also displacing or absorbing the thinly scattered Dorset descendants of the Small Tool people. The Canadian Thule culture carried the Inuit language to Greenland, while Thule-related groups in Alaska spread forms of the closely related Yupik language around the Bering Sea coast and to the North Pacific.

For the next few centuries, a warming climate reduced the formation of winter pack ice. Most Arctic communities relied on excursions inland for caribou, river and lake fish, and other resources during the short summer months. Some people also pursued whales during those animals' migrations, and all of them made use of resources such as nonmigratory seals in both summer and winter. After about 1400 CE, a period of increasing cold caused the peoples of northern Canada to give up permanent winter settlements, shifting instead to a nomadic seasonal round. This typically included warm-weather caribou hunting and river fishing, activities during which people

ULTIMA THULE

The term Ultima Thule has ancient origins and was used by early geographers and mapmakers to designate the northernmost part of the habitable ancient world. In literature, it also typically bears the sense of remoteness. References to Ultima Thule in modern literature appear in works by Edgar Allan Poe, Henry Wadsworth Longfellow, and the Australian writer Henry Handel Richardson.

lived in tents, and cold-weather seal hunting through the sea ice (at the animals' breathing holes), undertaken while people resided in snow houses—essentially the stereotypical way of life that characterizes all traditional Eskimo peoples. Because the climate shift was less extreme in areas closer to the coasts of the Pacific (including the Bering Sea) and Atlantic oceans, communities in those areas perpetuated the stable oceanside life established in the Thule period, building permanent dwellings of sod, logs, and stones. They rarely used snow houses except during winter travel, and they hunted through the sea ice chiefly in times of winter famine when stores of other foods had been exhausted.

COLONIZATION AND CONTEMPORARY DEVELOPMENTS

European explorers colonized the American Arctic as they moved through this vast area. The following passages reflect on the colonization of Greenland's coasts, western and southwestern Alaska, and the Arctic Ocean and Hudson Bay.

THE COASTS OF GREENLAND

In 986 CE brawny, red-bearded Erik the Red established a Norse settlement in a frozen wasteland he named Greenland. However, it may not have been until the 13th century that the Norse and Thule came into contact. Early in the 15th century, the Norse colony was abandoned when a general climatic cooling trend probably made subsistence farming impractical in the area. European fishermen built seasonally used base camps on Greenland's southern coasts during the 16th and 17th centuries. During the periods of European absence, Inuit peoples sometimes burned the seemingly abandoned buildings to simplify the collection of iron nails and metal fittings. These were easily transformed into implements that proved more durable than traditional stone tools. This destruction of fishing camps created tensions between the Europeans and the Inuit. The groups sometimes fought, but apparently there were no attempts at political domination.

In 1721 a permanent Danish-Norwegian colony was founded on Greenland. Its goals were missionization and trade. Unusually, the region's indigenous peoples were from the first treated as full citizens of the kingdom. Epidemics of European diseases struck almost immediately, killing as many as a third of the people on the island. In 1776 the Danish government granted a trade monopoly to the Royal Greenlandic Trading Company. With the restriction of contact with outsiders, losses to epidemic

Godthåb Fjord on the coast of Nuuk, Greenland. ©www.istockphoto.com/Mlenny Photography

disease were greatly reduced. Denmark retained a trading monopoly with Greenland until 1951.

Indigenous languages remained in general use after colonization. Because missionaries often learned Inuit while residing in Nuuk (now the capital city) and then left for more distant locales, the Nuuk dialect came into common use throughout Greenland. This helped create a sense of ethnic unity among indigenous Greenlanders, and that unity continued to grow with the 1861 publication of the first Inuit-language newspaper, *Atuagagdliutit* (an invented word originally meaning "distributed reading matter" or "free newspaper"). By the late 19th century, Greenland's native peoples had created a significant and growing vernacular literature and a name for their shared identity, Kalaaleq ("Greenland Inuk"; Inuk is the local ethnonym for someone who is a member of an Inuit-speaking group).

In 1862 Greenland was granted limited local self-government. In the period from 1905 to 1929, its residents shifted from a traditional subsistence economy to sheep breeding and cod fishing (although hunting remained important in the early 21st century). Schools also began to teach Danish. In 1953, after more than 200 years as a colony, Greenland became an integral part of Denmark and gained representation in the national legislative assembly. In 1979 Greenland achieved home rule, and in 2008 voters approved a referendum that granted it greater autonomy.

The Inuit Institute, Greenland's first institution of higher education, was formed in 1983. In 1989 it was reorganized as a university, Ilisimatusarfik, and became one of the few institutions dedicated to the study of Kalaaleq traditional cultures and languages. Within Greenland, university training in other subjects is still limited. As younger Kalaaleq commonly speak Danish as a second language, many enroll in Danish universities.

ALASKA'S SOUTHERN AND SOUTHWESTERN TERRITORIES

Vitus Bering set off on a voyage for the northern Pacific in 1728. Peter I (the Great) had planned the expedition back in 1724 to investigate the possibility of a passage between Siberia and North America. Failing this, he wanted to explore the viability of a passable sea route between the mercantile hubs of western Russia and China. Although poor visibility limited the results of this voyage, ensuing Russian explorations determined that the Pacific coast of North America was home to a seemingly inexhaustible population of sea otters. Russian entrepreneurs quickly seized on the opportunity to garner sea otter pelts, known for their lush feel and superior insulating qualities, as these were at the time almost the only items for which the Chinese were willing to engage in trade with Russia.

Russian rule was established in the region quickly and often brutally. Perhaps the worst atrocities occurred in 1745, when a large party of Russian and Siberian hunters overwintered in the Aleutian Islands. Members of the party engaged in such wholesale murder and sexual assault that they were later charged in the Russian courts and punished. Similar incidents of violent conquest occurred throughout the region, and over the next several decades the indigenous population was forced into virtual slavery. Russian administrators recognized native expertise in capturing sea otters and so negotiated with the hunters during the first part of the colonial era (albeit on an unequal basis given the colonizers' imposing firepower). However, these more or less voluntary levels of fur production proved inadequate for commercial trading. By 1761 the Russians had instituted a village-based quota system. They remained unsatisfied with the results and soon took entire villages hostage as a way to ensure the docility of

Aleut and Yupik men, nearly all of whom were impressed into service as hunters.

This created intense hardship for the elders, women, and children left behind. Hunting had provided most of their subsistence, and, with the hunters away or exhausted, several communities suffered from malnourishment or starvation in addition to the epidemic diseases that characterized European conquest throughout the Americas. Within a century of initial contact, the Aleut-speaking population had declined to no more than 2,000. At least 80 percent of their original number were gone. Around Kodiak Island and the Pacific coast, the decrease in roughly the same period was to about 3,000, a loss of about two-thirds. On the Bering Sea, where the fur trade was less intense, the loss was limited to about one-third or one-half of the population, all of it coming in the 19th century.

In 1799 the Russian-American Company was granted what amounted to governance of the Russian colonies in the North Pacific. The company undertook a period of expansion and eventually ruled thousands of miles of coast, from the Bering Sea to northern California. Russian Orthodox missionaries arrived at about the same time. They observed the brutalities committed against indigenous peoples, reported these to the tsar, and worked to ameliorate the horrendous conditions in the hostage villages. Although protective language was placed in the company's second charter, enforcement was haphazard. Nonetheless, and perhaps because the priests were clearly their advocates, many Aleuts and Yupiit converted to Orthodox Christianity.

The U.S. government purchased Russian America in 1867 and subsequently imposed its assimilationist policies on Native Alaskans. Various forms of pressure were applied to ensure that native communities shifted from subsistence to wage labour, from the use of their own languages to English, and from Russian Orthodox traditions to mainline Protestantism, among other things.

As elsewhere in the United States, these policies undermined indigenous traditions and generally caused local economies to shift from self-sufficiency and sustainability to a reliance on outside capital. As the sea otter neared extinction, some Yupik and Aleut communities shifted to the hunting of other fur-bearing mammals, such as seals and Arctic foxes. As among the neighbouring Northwest Coast Indians, other groups used their knowledge of local fisheries to ensure employment. These strategies met with various levels of success, but the native communities often faced circumstantial difficulties: demand for furs collapsed during the Great Depression of the 1930s, and fishermen had to cope with natural cycles in the population levels of various kinds of fish, the vagaries of consumer taste, and competition from better-equipped Euro-Americans.

By the mid-20th century, international politics were also affecting large numbers of indigenous Alaskans. World War II saw the removal of whole Native Alaskan communities under the aegis of protection and national defense. After the war, having in some cases endured years of difficult "temporary" conditions, those who returned to their homes found them in disrepair and in some cases ransacked. The Cold War ensured that the military presence in Alaska would continue to grow until the late 20th century. New facilities were often placed on property that indigenous groups used and regarded as their own, creating further hardships.

NORTHERN ALASKA AND CANADA

The area from the Bering Strait on north and east to the Mackenzie River remained unaffected by Russians until the middle of the 19th century, when Euro-American and

European whalers infested the region, bringing with them unknown germs and alcohol. As a result of these imports, native populations decreased by two-thirds or more in the short span between 1850 and 1910. In far northern Canada, the impact was lessened somewhat, for contact was limited and the thinly distributed populations more easily avoided the spread of disease. Nevertheless, European whalers active in Hudson Bay and elsewhere were a source of disease and disruption that resulted in a significant decline in native population in the 19th century.

Intensive whaling, and later the hunting of walruses, depleted some major food sources of far northern communities and in some cases created localized hardship. However, whalers often recognized the technical skills of the northern Yupiit and the Inuit and arranged for various kinds of partnership. A Euro-American might reside with a local family for a winter, gaining food, shelter, and company while the family would gain labour-saving technology, such as metal knives, steel needles, and rifles.

Widespread difficulties arose with the imposition of assimilationist policies by the United States and Canada and later, after the discovery of gold, oil, and mineral resources in the region. By the late 19th century, church-sponsored experiments in reindeer herding were promoting assimilation in northern Alaska. These ventures generally failed because of their incompatibility with the local culture. People were accustomed to moving widely across the landscape but also had the habit of returning frequently to their home communities, a practice that quickly caused overgrazing near settlements. In addition, Euro-American entrepreneurs generally had enough capital to crowd out native reindeer operations. Gold strikes on Canada's Klondike River in 1896 and near Nome, Alaska, in 1898 shifted attention away from indigenous economic development, incidentally providing many northern Native

The Klondike River gold strike of 1896 drew focus away from indigenous economic development. Hulton Archive/Getty Images

Alaskans with a welcome opportunity to return to traditional modes of subsistence.

As in western and southwestern Alaska, the northern parts of Alaska and Canada saw an increase in military facilities during and after World War II. By the 1950s and '60s, concerns about environmental degradation and land seizures caused Native Alaskans to file lawsuits to halt the development of oil and other resources. These suits eventually led to the Alaska Native Claims Settlement Act of 1971, in which the United States agreed to provide to Alaskan natives some $962.5 million and 44 million acres of land, all to be administered through native-run corporations. For administrative purposes and to encourage local development, the state was divided among 12 regional native corporations (seven of them Inuit or Yupik, one Aleut, and the rest Indian), each including a series of village corporations in which individual natives were sole shareholders. A 13th corporation serves Native Alaskans who reside outside the state. The corporations have promoted housing, local schools, satellite communications facilities, medical facilities, and programs directed at alcohol abuse. In addition, corporations have provided a training ground for native politicians active in state government, where they represent an increasingly sophisticated native citizenry.

Canada did not seek direct rule over the northern coastal region until the early 20th century, and the Canadian Inuit have had the same opportunities to vote and hold office as other Canadians only since about 1960 — a time that coincides with the creation of increasingly stable settlements, the extension of social welfare, a decline in the importance of the traditional hunting economy, and the beginnings of native organizations that seek the recognition of the Inuit as a distinct people with rights of self-governance and to lands and traditional culture.

Canada's Inuit proved quite adept at effecting political change. In the mid-1970s, the province of Quebec took from the dominion government all political responsibility for relationships with Inuit residing there. Inuit communities soon organized into village corporations with defined rights to land and resources. At about the same time, the Northwest Territories elected people of aboriginal descent to a majority of the 15 seats then in the territorial legislative assembly. In 1979 the first Inuit was elected to one of the two Northwest Territories seats in the national House of Commons. A proposal to divide the Northwest Territories into two parts, the eastern to include the major Inuit territory, was submitted to a plebiscite in 1982. The proposal won heavily in the east but only narrowly overall. It eventually passed, and what had been the eastern part of the Northwest Territories became the territory of Nunavut in 1999.

CONTEMPORARY DEVELOPMENTS

Indigenous American Arctic populations were rejuvenated throughout the 1900s. Better health care following the Second World War decreased the occurrence of infections, allowing populations to double in size from 1950 to 1980. Estimates of early 21st-century populations suggested that the total population of persons self-identified as Inuit, Yupik, or Aleut stood at about 130,000 individuals in Canada and the United States, with approximately 45,000 additional individuals in Greenland.

For native peoples throughout the Arctic, a key development from the late 20th century onward has been their sophisticated activism and increasing transnationalism. They were heavily involved in the broad global push for indigenous, or "Fourth World," rights that had begun by the late 1960s and was encouraged by the civil rights movements of the so-called First World and the new independence of the formerly colonized Third World. In 1977 the Inuit Circumpolar Conference was formed by the Inuit peoples of Greenland, Canada, and Alaska. In 1983 it was recognized officially by the United Nations. By the early 21st century it represented some 150,000 individuals of Inuit and Yupik heritage, including those of Siberia. The Aleut International Association, a sister group, formed in 1998. These organizations are particularly active in promoting the preservation of indigenous cultures and languages and in protecting the northern environment from global warming and resource exploitation. They are two of the six indigenous associations and eight member states with permanent membership status in the Arctic Council, an international forum for intergovernmental research, cooperation, and advocacy that works frequently with the United Nations.

The peoples who have managed to survive the
extreme conditions of the Arctic have a number of
similarities. These features are examined in detail in the
following chapter.

LINGUISTIC MAKEUP

Eskimo and Aleut, once neighbour languages on the
Alaska Peninsula, are related but quite distinct; together
they form the Eskimo-Aleut language family. Several
proposed relationships between Eskimo-Aleut and
other language families, such as Chukotko-Kamchatkan,
Uralic, and Indo-European, remain unconvincing.

The Eskimo division is further subdivided into Inuit
and Yupik. Inuit, or Eastern Eskimo (in Greenland called
Greenlandic or Kalaaleq; in Canada, Inuktitut; in Alaska,
Inupiaq), is a single language formed of a series of inter-
grading dialects that extend thousands of miles, from
eastern Greenland to northern Alaska and around the
Seward Peninsula to Norton Sound. There it adjoins
Yupik, or Western Eskimo. The Yupik section, however,
consists of five separate languages that were not mutu-
ally intelligible. Three of these are Siberian: Sirenikski is
now virtually extinct; Naukanski is restricted to the east-
ernmost Chukchi Peninsula; and Chaplinski is spoken on
Alaska's St. Lawrence Island, on the southern end of the
Chukchi Peninsula, and near the mouth of the Anadyr
River in the south and on Wrangel Island in the north.
In Alaska, Central Alaskan Yupik includes dialects that

covered the Bering Sea coast from Norton Sound to the Alaska Peninsula, where it met Pacific Yupik (known also as Sugpiaq or Alutiiq). Pacific Yupik comprises three dialects: that of the Kodiak Island group, that of the south shore of the Kenai Peninsula, and that of Prince William Sound.

Aleut now includes only a single language of two dialects, but, before the disruption that followed the 18th-century arrival of Russian fur hunters, it included several dialects, if not separate languages, spoken from about longitude 158° W on the Alaska Peninsula, throughout the Aleutian Islands, and westward to Attu, the westernmost island of the Aleutian chain. The Russians transplanted some Aleuts to formerly unoccupied islands of the Commander group, west of the Aleutians, and to those of the Pribilofs, in the Bering Sea.

KAYAK AND UMIAK

The English language has freely adopted several words taken from Arctic material culture, including *kayak* (*qayaq*) and *umiak* (*umiaq*). The kayak is a common type of canoe that originated with the Inuit of Greenland and was later also used by Alaskan Eskimos. It has a pointed bow and stern and no keel and is covered except for a cockpit in which the paddler or paddlers sit, facing forward and using a double-bladed paddle. The kayak was commonly built for one occupant but could be designed for two or three. Arctic peoples built kayaks by stretching seal or other animal skins over a driftwood or whalebone frame and rubbing them with animal fat to waterproof the covering. The paddler wore an overlapping shield to permit the kayak to be righted without shipping (i.e., taking on) water after rolling over. Originally, the kayak was used by men for fishing and hunting. The kayak's shallow draft, narrow width, and quiet operation allowed hunters to explore tightly constricted waterways with great stealth, which helped them harvest more game. For purposes of hunting, the kayak was gradually abandoned in the 20th century in favour of motorboats. Today kayaks are made of several materials and in many varieties, and they are chiefly used for recreation and sport. They are known for their comfort and controllability.

The umiak, also known as the woman's boat, was used by the Greenland Inuit and later by the Alaskan Eskimos for the purpose of transport, rather than hunting or fishing. Like the kayak, the umiak was made of seal or other animal skins stretched over a driftwood or whalebone frame and was paddled. Unlike the kayak, it was an open boat, either round in shape or elongated much like the birchbark canoe. The umiak was used mostly by women for transporting themselves, children, the elderly, and possessions. But it was also used by men for whaling. In the 20th century, the umiak was first furnished with an outboard motor and finally displaced (like the kayak) by conventional motorboats, except for recreation.

Kayaking. Dennis Curran/Vermont Department of Tourism and Marketing

CLASSIFICATION OF ETHNIC GROUPS

Generally, rather than organizing themselves into clans or tribes, the American Eskimos traditionally identified their groups by the location in which they lived. The suffix -*miut* ("people of") was applied in a nesting set of labels to persons of any specifiable place—from the home of a family or two to a broad region with myriad residents. Among the largest of the customary -*miut* designators are those coinciding at least roughly with the limits of a dialect or subdialect, the speakers of which tended to seek spouses from within that group. Such groups might range in size from 200 to perhaps 1,000 people.

Historically, each individual's identity was defined on the basis of connections such as kinship and marriage in addition to place and language. All of these continued to be important to Arctic self-identity in the 20th and 21st centuries, although native peoples in the region have also formed large—and in some cases pan-Arctic—organizations to facilitate their representation in legal and political affairs.

Ethnographies, historical accounts, and documents from before the late 20th century typically used geographic nomenclature to refer to groups that shared similar dialects, customs, and material cultures. For instance, in reference to groups residing on the North Atlantic and Arctic coasts, these texts might discuss the East Greenland Eskimo, West Greenland Eskimo, and Polar Eskimo, although only the last territorial division corresponded to a single self-contained, in-marrying (endogamous) group. The peoples of Canada's North Atlantic and eastern Hudson Bay were referred to as the Labrador Eskimo and the Eskimo of Quebec. These were often described as whole units, although each comprises a number of separate societies. The inhabitants of Baffinland were often included in the Central Eskimo, a grouping that otherwise included the Caribou Eskimo of the barrens west of Hudson Bay and the Iglulik, Netsilik, Copper, and Mackenzie Eskimo, all of whom live on or near the Arctic Ocean in northern Canada. The Mackenzie Eskimo, however, are also set apart from other Canadians as speakers of the western, or Inupiaq, dialect of the Inuit (Eastern Eskimo) language. Descriptions of these Alaskan Arctic peoples have tended to be along linguistic rather than geographic lines and include the Inupiaq-speaking Inupiat, who live on or near the Arctic Ocean and as far south as the Bering Strait. All the groups noted thus far reside near open water that freezes solid in winter, speak dialects of the Inuit language, and are commonly referred to in aggregate as Inuit (meaning "the people").

The Yupik and other Arctic peoples took advantage of the good fishing along inland rivers, such as the Yukon. © Nomad/SuperStock

ARCTIC CLOTHING

The clothing of the Arctic peoples is adapted to the Arctic cold. It was made from animal skins, but because of the climate it was sewn and tailored to the body to keep out the wind. The fur or pelt of the animal was retained, and garments were usually worn fur side in. Thread was of animal sinew, awls for piercing the skin were generally stone, and needles were of bone or ivory. Arctic peoples used all available animal skins: polar bear, deer, caribou reindeer, antelope, dog, and fox. They also used birds—the skin for clothing and the feathers as decoration. Sealskin was ideal for boots, which were made with the fur turned inward. Seal gut was used to make waterproof outer garments for those who ventured onto the sea.

Both sexes wore the same type of garments: a hooded tunic or coat, trousers, and boots. The hooded tunic was variously named in different areas. Two of these—the parka of the Aleutian Islands and the anorak of Greenland—have become essential items of winter clothing in all regions where cold weather prevails.

The other American Arctic groups live farther south, where open water is less likely to freeze solid for greatly extended periods. The Bering Sea Eskimo and St. Lawrence Island Eskimo live around the Bering Sea, where resources include migrating sea mammals and, in the mainland rivers, seasonal runs of salmon and other fish. The Pacific Eskimo, however, live on the shores of the North Pacific itself, around Kodiak Island and Prince William Sound, where the Alaska Current prevents open water from freezing at all. Each of these three groups speaks a distinct form of Yupik. Together they are commonly referred to as Yupik Eskimo or as Yupiit ("the people").

In the Gulf of Alaska, ethnic distinctions were blurred by Russian colonizers who used the term Aleut to refer not only to people of the Aleutian Islands but also to the culturally distinct groups residing on Kodiak Island and the neighbouring areas of the mainland. As a result, many modern native people from Kodiak, the Alaska Peninsula, and Prince William Sound identify themselves as Aleuts, although only those from the tip of the peninsula and the Aleutian Islands are descended from people who spoke what linguists refer to as the Aleut language. These latter refer to themselves as Unangan ("people"). The groups from Kodiak Island and the neighbouring areas traditionally spoke the form of Yupik called Pacific Yupik, Sugpiaq, or Alutiiq and refer to themselves as Alutiiq (singular) or Alutiit (plural).

ARCTIC TRADITIONAL CULTURES

The traditional cultures of the Arctic tend to be examined in two general groups. The first includes northern Yupiit and the Inuit, seasonally migratory peoples who reside on or near coastlines that freeze in winter. The second group comprises the more sedentary southern Yupiit and Aleuts, who live on or near areas of open water along the coast of the Pacific Ocean.

THE SEASONAL MIGRATIONS OF THE NORTHERN YUPIIT AND THE INUIT

The northern Yupiit and the Inuit organized their economies by season. By following the patterns of their forebears, the Thules, they mainly harvested the resources of both the land and sea.

HUNTING

Traditional peoples generally followed the Thule subsistence pattern, in which summers were spent in pursuit of caribou and fish and other seasons were devoted to the pursuit of sea mammals, especially seals. Food was also stored for consumption during the deepest part of winter.

There were exceptions to this pattern, however. People of the Bering Strait islands, for instance, depended almost entirely on sea mammals, walrus being the most important. In the specialized Alaskan whaling villages between the Seward Peninsula and Point Barrow, caribou and seals were outweighed as food resources by bowhead whales (*Baleana mysticetus*). In the Brooks Range of northern Alaska, some people were year-round caribou hunters who also depended on traded sea-mammal oil as a condiment and a source of heat. In the Barren Grounds, west of Hudson Bay, some groups used no sea products at all, illuminating their snow houses with burning caribou fat and heating these homes with twig fires.

Whaling umiaks carried a professional crew that was directed by the boat's owner, or umialik. Emory Kristof/National Geographic Image Collection/Getty Images

The bow and arrow were the standard tools of land hunters. Seals and walrus were taken from shore with a thrown harpoon tipped with a toggling head—an asymmetrical point with a line affixed, shaped to twist sidewise in the wound as the detachable shaft pulled loose. Kayak-based seal hunters used specialized harpoons with fixed barbs rather than toggling heads. These were often cast with the spear-thrower or throwing board, a flat trough of wood that cradled the butt of the dart and formed an extension of the thrower's arm, increasing the velocity of the thrown projectile. The whaling umiak was manned by a professional crew. It was directed by the boat's owner, or *umialik*, and a marksman who wielded a heavy harpoon with a detachable toggling head and line attached to sealskin floats. In Quebec, whales were harpooned from kayaks or run aground in shallow bays.

SHELTER

Most shelter in winter was in substantial semisubterranean houses of stone or sod over wooden or whalebone frameworks. In Alaska, save for the far north, heat was provided by a central wood fire that was placed beneath a smoke hole. Throughout the north and in Greenland, a large sea-mammal oil lamp served the same purpose. In 19th-century Siberia and on St. Lawrence Island, the older semisubterranean house was given up for a yurt-like structure with sod walls and a walrus-hide roof.

The people nearest the Arctic Ocean relied on the snow house in winter, with most groups moving onto fresh ice fields in search of seals during that season. Caribou hunters and lake and river fishermen used the snow house on land. The caribou specialists of northern Alaska often lived through the winter in double-layered dome-shaped tents, heated like the coastal snow houses with an oil lamp. These dwellings commonly housed an

IGLOOS

Canadian and Greenland Inuit (Eskimos) use an igloo (iglu), or *aputiak*, as a provisional residence during the winter or lodging on their hunting ground. The word *igloo* stems from *igdlu*, the Eskimo word for "house." The word is related to the town of Iglulik and the Inuit people known as the Iglulirmiut (literally "people of the place with houses"), both on the island of Iglulik. The igloo, usually made from blocks of snow and dome-shaped, is used only in the area between the Mackenzie River delta and Labrador where, in the summer, Inuit live in sealskin or, more recently, cloth tents.

To build the igloo, the builder takes a deep snowdrift of fine-grained, compact snow and cuts it into blocks with a snow knife, a swordlike instrument originally made of bone but now usually of metal. Each block is a rectangle measuring about 2 feet by 4

Eskimos build domed winter shelters, known as igloos, from blocks of snow. James Balog/Stone/Getty Images

feet (60 cm by 120 cm) and 8 inches (20 cm) thick. After a first row of these blocks has been laid out in a circle on a flat stretch of snow, the top surfaces of the blocks are shaved off in a sloping angle to form the first rung of a spiral. Additional blocks are added to the spiral to draw it inward until the dome is completed except for a hole left at the top for ventilation. Joints and crevices are filled with loose snow. A clear piece of ice or seal intestine is inserted for a window. A narrow, semicylindrical passageway about 10 feet (3 metres) long, with vaults for storing supplies, leads into the igloo. Drafts are kept from the main room by a sealskin flap hung over the exterior entrance to the passageway and by a low, semicircular retaining wall that is sometimes built out a few feet from the end of the tube. The major furnishings are a shallow saucer to burn seal blubber for heat and light and a low sleeping platform of snow covered with willow twigs topped by caribou furs.

The dimensions of igloos vary, but they generally accommodate only one family. An experienced Inuit can build a snow igloo in between one and two hours. Sod, stone, and wood have also been used to construct igloos.

extended family. In East and West Greenland, communal dwellings were built of stone, housed up to 50 people from different kin groups, and were arranged such that each nuclear family had its own interior space and oil lamp. Communities in the far north of Greenland chose to use smaller stone houses designed to shelter nuclear families.

Among the Yupiit a special large semisubterranean house, called a *kashim* by the Russians, was used for public and ceremonial occasions and as a men's residence. The *kashim* was the place where men built their boats, repaired their equipment, took sweat baths, educated young boys, and hosted community dances. Women had their own homes in which they worked and cared for their children.

Winter shelter often consisted of a whalebone or wooden framework covered with sod or stone. Steven Kazlowski/Science Faction/Getty Images

In many cases the women's homes were connected to one another and to the *kashim* by a system of tunnels, not all of them generally known. A number of folktales tell how canny women saved their families from raids by directing them to hidden tunnels that opened far away from the village.

The institution of the *kashim* was stronger to the south of the Bering Strait than to its north. *Kashims* did not exist on St. Lawrence Island or in Siberia, nor were they found east of Point Barrow until the late 19th or early 20th century, when they began to be used by Inuit living near the Mackenzie River.

TRANSPORTATION

Both the single-cockpit kayak and the larger open umiak were virtually universal, although they were not used the

SLED DOGS

The breeds most commonly used in Arctic climates to pull a sled across snow and ice are the Siberian husky, Alaskan Malamute, Samoyed, Eskimo dog, and Laika. They are all large, powerful dogs with thick coats and high endurance.

On the North American continent a "fan hitch" (where each of 12 to 15 dogs was separately attached to the sled by its own lead) was used to carry both people and supplies. Now a team, usually of 8 dogs, in a "pair hitch" (double file and side by side) is the most common. In the Siberian regions of Russia, smaller teams are used.

Alaskan Malamute. © Kent & Donna Dannen

same way everywhere. The kayak was generally used as a seal-hunting craft, but, in the places where open-water sealing was limited, it was used to intercept migrating caribou as they crossed lakes and rivers. The umiak was usually a freight vessel, often rowed by women facing backward, but in whaling and walrus-hunting regions it was used as a hunting boat and paddled by a male crew facing forward. Winter transport was by sled, pulled by dogs or by both dogs and people. In most regions the number of sled dogs—which ate the same food as humans and thus were a burden in times of want—was limited, an exception being the few areas in which relative plenty was provided by whales or migrating salmon.

SOCIAL ORGANIZATION

The flexibility of movement required by the seasonally varied subsistence quest was supported by the flexible organization of society. Individuals obtained psychological and material support from their kindred and tended to avoid people who were not kin, but there were devices for creating kinlike relationships that could extend the social and territorial sphere in which an individual could move in safety and comfort. These included a variety of institutionalized relationships. People bearing the same name as a relative might be treated as if they held the same relation, and trading partners, song partners, meat-sharing partners, and partners created by the temporary exchange of spouses might also be treated approximately as relatives.

Generally, American Eskimo recognized kin on both the paternal and maternal sides of the family to about the degree of second cousin. Marriage with cousins was frowned upon by most groups although permitted by some. Certain groups also emphasized paternal kin over maternal. On St. Lawrence Island and in Siberia, however, there were patrilineal clans—named groups of all people related in the male line. In Siberia marriage could not be contracted by two members of the same clan, although on St. Lawrence such a rule was not enforced.

There the walrus- and whale-hunting crews were composed of clansmen, the senior male became clan chief, and the chief of the strongest local clan acted as the village chief.

Among other groups there was no formal position of chief, the closest to an exception being the *umialik* of the Inupiat. In addition to owning the boat used for whaling, the *umialik* was the employer of a whaling crew, recruiting his men for their professional ability and acting as benefactor to them and their families. In many villages each *umialik* and his crew controlled a *kashim*. The title of *umialik* was also used in some villages not devoted to whaling, especially in the northern Alaskan interior, where the *umialik* was the organizer of a caribou-hunting team. The position of *umialik* was not inherited but was gained by skilled entrepreneurs, and it brought no control over anyone but the *umialik*'s own crew (and then only to the extent that an individual chose to remain a crew member). South of the Bering Strait the title was rarely used.

RELIGION

Religious beliefs were based on animism. All things—animate or otherwise—were believed to have a living essence. Thus, all humans, animals, plants, and objects had souls or spirits, which might be related to one another in a hereafter, details of the location of which varied from group to group. Courtesies given to freshly killed animals promoted their reincarnation as new animals of the same species. The souls of humans were subject to interference from other spirits, and soul loss meant illness or even death. There also were ideas of human reincarnation. The name of a deceased person was given to a child who "became" that person by being addressed with kinship terms appropriate to the deceased.

Traditionally, all people were in contact with the spirit world. They carried amulets of traditional or individual potency, experienced dreams, devised songs or other words of power, and achieved special relationships with particular spirit-beings. Men and women who were especially adept at such contact became shamans. They were called on to cure the sick by recovering lost soul-stuff, to foretell the future, to determine the location of game, and so forth—all with the help of powerful spirit familiars.

Shamans were also expected to contact a few more strongly personified spirit-beings, such as the female being (whose name and attributes varied from group to group) who governed important land or sea mammals. When game was scarce, the shaman might cajole her into providing more bounty. In Greenland the shaman was also an entertainer whose séances, escape tricks, and noisy spirit helpers could enliven a long winter's night in the communal house.

SEDENTARY PEOPLES: THE SOUTHERN YUPIIT AND THE ALEUTS

Much like that of the nearby Northwest Coast Indians, the southern Yupiit and the Aleuts culled their foods and material culture almost entirely from the sea. Additionally, they used some of the same techniques as the northern Yupiit and the Inuit: sod-covered and semisubterranean houses, kayaks and umiaks wrapped in skins, and tools for fishing and hunting. Their hierarchical society was made up of formal chiefs (evidently passed down through the male line), other elites, commoners, and a class of slaves

WALRUS

The early cultures of the American Arctic hunted a variety of animals, among them the walrus. A huge, seal-like mammal, it inhabits Arctic seas. There are two subspecies: the Atlantic walrus (*Odobenus rosmarus rosmarus*) and the Pacific walrus (*O. rosmarus divergens*). Male Pacific walrus are slightly larger than the Atlantic variety, and they have longer tusks.

The grayish skin of the walrus is 1–2 inches (2–4 centimetres) thick, with deep folds around the shoulders. The skin is covered with short reddish hair, giving the animals an overall cinnamon colour. The walrus has a rounded head, small eyes, and no external ears. Its muzzle is short and broad and has a conspicuous moustache of stiff, quill-like whiskers (vibrissae). The male, which reaches a maximum length and weight of about 12 feet (3.7 metres) and 3,700 pounds (1,700 kilograms), is about a third larger than the female.

Both sexes possess long tusks (the upper canine teeth) that project downward from the mouth. In the male they can grow

Walrus. © Royalty-Free/Corbis

to about a metre in length and 12 pounds (5.4 kg) in weight. The tusks function mainly in mating display and in defense against other walrus. They are not used to dig food from the ocean floor. The walrus feeds at depths of less than 260 feet (80 m), usually at 30–160 feet (10–50 m). Rooting along the ocean floor with its snout, it identifies prey with its whiskers. The walrus's diet consists largely of clams and mussels but occasionally includes fish and even small seals.

The walrus is valued by both the Inuit and commercial hunters for blubber, hide, and ivory tusks. Its numbers have been reduced by commercial operations. Walrus are now protected from sealers but are still subject to subsistence hunting by aboriginals. Like seals, the walrus is a pinniped (fin-footed mammal). It is the sole living member of the family Odobenidae.

that was generally composed of war captives. Although the Yupik-speaking people of the Kodiak region maintained *kashims* that seem to have functioned generally like those of the north and were said to be "owned" by local chiefs, the Aleut-speaking groups had no similar structure. Unfortunately, the region's conquest by Russian fur hunters eradicated many details of indigenous life before they could be thoroughly recorded.

American Subarctic peoples are those who traditionally reside in Alaskan and Canadian areas of the Subarctic. Subarctic Canadians are identified to as First Nations peoples, and Alaskans are known as Native Alaskans.

The Subarctic is dominated by the taiga, or boreal forest, an ecosystem of coniferous forest and large marshes. Subarctic peoples traditionally used a variety of technologies to cope with the cold northern winters and were adept

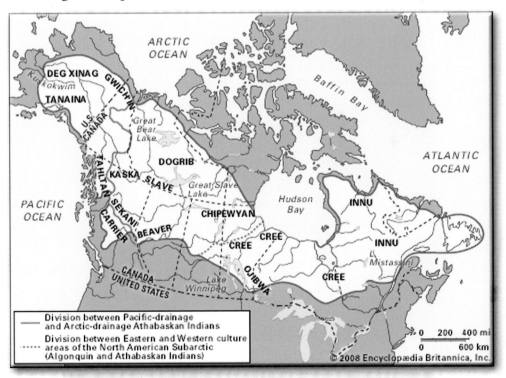

Distribution of American Subarctic cultures.

in the production of well-insulated homes, fur garments, toboggans, ice chisels, and snowshoes. The traditional diet included game animals such as moose, caribou, bison (in the southern locales), beaver, and fish, as well as wild plant foods such as berries, roots, and sap. Food resources were distributed quite thinly over the subarctic landscape, and starvation was always a potential problem.

By the 1600s European fur traders had recognized that the taiga provided an optimal climate for the production of dense pelts. These traders decisively influenced the region's indigenous peoples, as did Christian missionaries. The fur trade had an especially strong impact on traditional economies, as time spent trapping furs could not be spent on direct subsistence activities. This caused a rather rapid increase in the use of purchased food items

Taiga (boreal forest), with white spruce, birch, and low shrubs, near the Fortymile River, a tributary of the Yukon River, east-central Alaska, U.S. Photograph © George Wuerthner

such as flour and sugar, which were substituted for wild fare. Despite much pressure to change, however, the relative isolation of the region has facilitated the persistence of many traditional beliefs, hunting customs, kinship relations, and the like.

The American Subarctic culture area contains two relatively distinct zones. The Eastern Subarctic is inhabited by speakers of Algonquian languages, including the Innu (formerly Montagnais and Naskapi) of northern Quebec, the Cree, and several groups of Ojibwa who, after the beginning of the fur trade, displaced the Cree from what are now west-central Ontario and eastern Manitoba. The Western Subarctic is largely home to Athabaskan speakers, whose territories extend from Canada into Alaska. Cultural differences among the Athabaskans justify the delineation of the Western Subarctic into two subareas. The first, drained mostly by the northward-flowing Mackenzie River system, is inhabited by the Chipewyan, Beaver, Slave, and Kaska nations. Their cultures were generally more mobile and less socially stratified than that of the second subarea, where salmon streams that drain into the Pacific Ocean provide a reliable food resource and natural gathering places. Its groups include the Carrier, part of the Gwich'in (Kutchin), the Tanaina, and the Deg Xinag.

Northward the Algonquians and Athabaskans border on the Inuit (Canadian Eskimo). To the west the Canadian Athabaskans encounter the Tlingit, Tsimshian, and other Northwest Coast Indians, while the Alaskan groups abut Yupik/Yupiit (American Eskimo) lands.

IDEOLOGY

Living in the Subarctic requires weathering its arduous environmental conditions. Thus, most Subarctic cultures placed high value on personal independence and responsibility. They viewed the world as generally hazardous and gave greater weight to concrete, current realities rather than future possibilities. In anticipation of potential scarcity, Subarctic cultural concepts included not only personal competence but also an acknowledgement of the individual's need to rely upon others and to place the well-being of the group ahead of personal gain.

Many Subarctic cultures cultivated personality traits such as reticence, emotionally undemonstrative interaction styles, deference to others, strong individual control of aggressive impulses, and the ability to bear up stoically to deprivation. Although hostility was not absent from traditional culture, most groups preferred that it be only indirectly revealed through such outlets as sorcery or gossip. Subarctic individuals' ease with long silences and preference for subdued emotional responses have sometimes been a source of cross-cultural misunderstanding with individuals from outside the region, who are often less taciturn.

TERRITORIAL ARRANGEMENT

Precontact peoples of the Subarctic traditionally survived by hunting and gathering. They shared a variety of cultural practices with other hunters and gatherers around the world, but their particular approaches and technologies were specifically modified for their northern habitation. Most northern societies were organized around nuclear, or sometimes three-generation, families. The next level of social organization, the band, comprised a few related couples, their dependent children, and their dependent elders. Bands generally included no more than 20 to 30 individuals, who lived, hunted, and traveled together.

Although Eastern Subarctic peoples traditionally identified with a particular geographic territory, they generally chose not to organize politically beyond the level of the band. Instead, they identified themselves as members of the same tribe or nation based on linguistic and kinship affinities they shared with neighbouring bands. Seasonal gatherings of several bands often occurred at good fishing lakes or near rich hunting grounds for periods that were as intensely sociable as they were abundantly provided with fish or game. The fur trade period created a new type of territorial group among these peoples, known as the home guard or trading-post band, usually named for the settlement in which its members traded. These new groups amalgamated the smaller bands and notably expanded the population in which marriage occurred.

In the Pacific drainage area, sedentary villages were the preferred form of geopolitical organization, each with an associated territory for hunting and gathering. On the lower Yukon and upper Kuskokwim rivers, Deg Xinag village life centred on the *kashim*, or men's house, where a council of male elders met to hear disputes and where elaborate seasonal ceremonies were performed.

Whether organized in bands or villages, individual leadership and authority derived primarily from the combination of eloquence, wisdom, experience, healing or magical power, generosity, and a capacity for hard work.

SETTLEMENT AND SHELTER

As a survival strategy, groups of varying sizes (families or bands) moved from one location to another a dictated by the changing seasons. In early winter, bands in northwest Canada hunted caribou throughout the mountains. In other areas, autumn drew people to the shorelines of lakes and bays where large numbers of ducks and geese could be taken for the winter larder. At other times people gathered around lakes to fish. In late winter the Deg Xinag quit their villages and headed for spring camps, as much for a change of scenery as for the good fishing.

As dependence on fur trapping became heavier, the Cree, Slave, Kaska, and many other groups developed a two-part annual cycle. In winter the family lived on its trapline. In summer the family brought its furs to the trading post and camped there until fall, enjoying abundant social interaction. The warm months with their long daylight became a time for visiting and often included dances (often to fiddle music), marriages, and appearances by the region's Anglican or Roman Catholic bishop.

Despite much movement, shelters were not always portable. The Deg Xinag spent winters in houses excavated in the soil, roofed with beams and poles, hung with mats, and provided with an entry. Other groups, such as the Cree and Ojibwa, built conical winter lodges durably roofed with boughs, earth, and snow. On the trail, however, people put up skin or brush shelters, simple lean-tos, or camped in the open facing a fire.

MATERIAL CULTURE

Traditional subsistence activities throughout the Subarctic were heavily influenced by a profusion of diverse weaponry, snares, and other clever technologies. Significant mechanisms abounded: the bow and arrow, with stone or bone tips for different kinds of game; lances; the spear-thrower (or atlatl) and spear; weirs and basket traps for fish; nets of willow bark and of other substances; snares for small game such as rabbits; deadfalls (traps with logs or other weights that fall on game and kill them); pit traps; and decoys for birds. Vehicles were

Cree birchbark container with scraped-surface motifs, c. 1870; in the Denver Art Museum. Courtesy of the Denver Art Museum

also vital, as people depended heavily on mobility for survival. These included bark canoes, hardwood toboggans, and travel aids such as large sinew-netted snowshoes to run down big game, a smaller variety to break trail for the toboggan, and snow goggles to use against the glare of the spring sun.

Because dog teams require large quantities of meat, they were not kept to pull toboggans until the fur trade period, when people began to supplement their diets with European staples. After that point, dog teams became increasingly important in transporting furs to market. An idea of the extent to which people depended on game and of the labour involved in obtaining adequate amounts of food can be gained from food-consumption figures obtained in the mid-20th century. In the relatively poor country west of James Bay, 400 Cree men, women, and children in the course of a fall, winter, and spring (nine months) consumed about 128,000 pounds (58,000 kg) of meat and fish in addition to staples from the store, especially flour, lard, and sugar.

Subarctic peoples augmented their technical resource-fulness and skill in hunting with magic and divination. A noteworthy form of divination used in locating game required heating a large animal's shoulder blade over fire until it cracked. Hunters then went in the direction of the crack. The random element in the method increased the chances that they would go to a fresh, relatively undisturbed piece of ground.

Across the Subarctic, people preserved meat by drying and pounding it together with fat and berries to make pemmican. The Pacific-drainage Athabaskans also preserved salmon by smoking. Other widely distributed technical skills included complicated chemical processes, as in using animal brains or human urine to tan caribou and moose skins. These were then sewn into garments with the help of bone needles and animal sinew. Women also plaited rabbit skins into ropes and wove roots to form watertight baskets.

SPEAR-THROWER

The spear-thrower (which is also called a throwing-stick, or atlatl) is a device usually consisting of a rod or board with a groove on the upper surface and a hook, thong, or projection at the rear end to hold the weapon in place until its release. Its purpose is to give greater velocity and force to the spear. In use from prehistoric times, the spear-thrower was necessary for the efficient felling of large animals, including the mammoth.

Usually constructed of wood, bamboo, bone, or antler, the spear-thrower performs the function of an extra joint in the arm. The spear lies along the spear-thrower, with its butt resting against a projecting peg or in the slight socket made by the septum of the node (in the case of bamboo devices). In the case of Arctic and Subarctic cultures, the spear-thrower was used for discharging harpoons and fish spears.

OWNERSHIP AND SOCIAL ORGANIZATION

Land and water, which supplied traditional Subarctic peoples with food, belonged to no single person or group. However, if a band was presently taking advantage of a berry patch, creek, or hunting range, nobody would commandeer the area. Garments, food reserves, and other portable goods were recognized as having individual owners. When in need, a group could borrow from another's food cache, provided the food was replaced and the owners told of the act as soon as possible. Legally inalienable family trapping territories came into being with the fur trade and in many places have been registered by the federal or dominion government. Sharing game was always important economically, while gifts other than food were bestowed primarily for ceremonial purposes.

Although social stratification was not customary across the entire Subarctic, the Deg Xinag informally recognized three classes of families. Usually at least three-quarters of a Deg Xinag village comprised common people. Rich families, which accumulated surplus food thanks to members' industry or superior hunting and fishing abilities, constituted about 5 percent of the community. They took the lead in the community's ceremonial life. The rest of the people did little and lived off the others. Consequently, they enjoyed so little respect that they had a hard time finding spouses.

RELATIONSHIPS AMONG FAMILY AND KIN

Families within a local group might include up to three generations: husband, wife, offspring—often including adopted children—and occasionally dependant elders.

Such groupings represented the time-honoured element of economic activity and emotional sanctuary. The family's powerful significance, particularly during childhood, is revealed in folklore about the unhappy lot of cruelly treated orphans. Children with neither parents nor grandparents suffered the worst.

Kinship in the Subarctic traditionally included some categories that are common in traditional cultures but less commonly observed in the 21st century. Parallel cousins, the children of one's mother's sisters or father's brothers, were usually called by the same kinship term as one's siblings and treated as such. In contrast, cross-cousins, the children of one's father's sisters or mother's brothers, were often seen as the best pool from which to draw a mate. Northern peoples held strong prohibitions against incest, which was traditionally defined as sexual contact between siblings (including parallel cousins), between parents and children, and between adjacent generations of in-laws (e.g., mothers-in-law and sons-in-law, fathers-in-law and daughters-in-law).

Kin relations among Subarctic peoples often involved a sort of emotional division of labour: supportive, teasing, or joking relationships occurred with one group of relatives, while authoritative, circumspect, or avoidance relationships were the norm with another group of kin. In many cases, and probably in support of the incest prohibition, the appropriate form of interaction was based on generational proximity: grandparents and grandchildren would tease, joke, hug, and cuddle, while interaction between adjacent generations (parent-child, sibling-sibling, parents-in-law and children-in-law) would be more reserved. In other cases the relationships were based on lineage. Casual interactions tended to be more common with relatives from the mother's line and avoidance relations more common with those from the father's line. Some groups combined both generational and lineal forms.

In following these customs, siblings of the opposite sex who had reached puberty generally conducted themselves circumspectly in each other's presence and even tended to practice polite avoidance, as did fathers and their grown daughters. Ceremonial avoidance also governed the relationship of a man and his mother-in-law, contrasting with the camaraderie linking brothers-in-law, which was one of the warmest of all relationships between grown men. Among the Kaska, for instance, a group that could joke freely, and even engage in sexual ribaldry, comprised a woman, her husband's brother, and her sister's husband (or alternatively, a man, his wife's sister, and his brother's wife).

Marriages in the Subarctic were traditionally founded upon an agreement between the parents of a potential bride and groom. The preferences of those to wed were taken into account, but obedience to parental choices was expected. The value placed on both women's and men's contributions in the difficult environment meant that a marriage usually entailed one of two kinds of social and economic exchange. Most typically, the groom would provide services to the bride's family for a period of time. The couple's residence with the wife's family provided emotional support as well as time to evaluate the husband's hunting prowess and ensured the wife's female kin were available to assist her in at least her first pregnancy and childbirth. Less often, two young women would exchange places, with a daughter from each family becoming daughter-in-law to the other family.

Although households were primarily monogamous, some marriages included one husband shared by two wives. This could happen, for example, when a man engaged in the levirate, a custom in which he espoused his dead brother's widow and took on the responsibility of providing for her and her children.

ENCULTURATION OF THE YOUNG

To protect the health and safety of mothers and children, traditional Subarctic cultures instituted assorted pregnancy prohibitions and postnatal rites. Mothers gave birth in their homes, in a building especially for birthing, or even out in the forest, as indicated by early travelers among the Mi'kmaq. One or more knowledgeable women helped the mother give birth and care for the delivered child. Swaddled babies were diapered with moss and carried on the mother's back in an ornamented skin bag or a cradleboard.

Family members and other relatives played the major role in the informal process of childhood education. A child had considerable scope to learn through copying others. Thus, a Kaska parent might say "Make tea!" and a small girl would try to reconstruct what she had often observed her mother and older sisters doing but what she had never been formally instructed to do. Parents did not neglect disciplining and even chastising a disobedient child for such offenses as stealing and rebelliousness. More important for the formation of personalities is the fact that parental treatment subtly but firmly encouraged children to become independent and self-reliant.

Several "firsts," including the first tooth, the first game killed by a boy, and a girl's first menstruation (menarche), were ceremonially recognized, sometimes by a small feast. Menarche was recognized by an elaborate series of ritual observances that were undertaken to protect the girl and her family from the powerful forces that were effecting the changes in her body. Athabaskan peoples paid the greatest ritual attention to menarche, with Gwich'in girls moving to a special shelter constructed some distance from the family camp and staying there for up to a year. At the menarche camp, a girl wore a pointed hood that caused her to look down toward the ground. Other ceremonial precautions included a rattle of bone that was supposed to prevent her from hearing anything, a special stick to use if she wanted to scratch her head, and a special cup that should not touch her lips. Subsequent menstruation involved only a short period of seclusion.

SPIRITUAL CONVICTIONS

Subarctic peoples tended to have a decidedly personal connection with the supernatural. It was common for young women and men to embark on a vision quest. They put a great deal of faith in one or even multiple guardian spirits for security and counsel. In Kaska terms the vision occurred by "dreaming of animals in a lonely place" or hearing "somebody sing," perhaps a moose in the guise of a person. Dreams notified an individual of impending events and might advise one how to behave to achieve success or avoid misfortune.

Among several Subarctic peoples there was a widespread belief that hunting success depended upon treating prey animals and their remains with reverence. This involved various practices such as disposing of the animals' bones carefully so that dogs could not chew them. Respect was particularly evident in the use of polite circumlocutions to refer to bears. Many groups undertook several ceremonial observances in bear hunting, including a purifying sweat bath before departing on the hunt and an offer of tobacco to a bear that had been killed. Afterward the people feasted and danced in its honour.

SHAMAN

The shaman is healer, priest, and psychopomp. That is to say, he cures sicknesses, directs communal sacrifices, and escorts the souls of the dead to the other world. He is able to do all this by virtue of his techniques of ecstasy (i.e., by his power to leave his body at will during a trancelike state). In Siberia and northeastern Asia, a person becomes a shaman by hereditary transmission of the shamanistic profession or by "election." More rarely a person can become a shaman by his own decision or upon the request of the clan, but self-made shamans are regarded as weaker than those who inherit the profession or are elected by a supernatural agency. In North America, however, the voluntary "quest" for shamanistic powers constitutes the principal method of selection. No matter how the selection takes place, a shaman is recognized as such only after a series of initiatory trials and the receipt of instructions from qualified masters.

The most important function of the shaman in all cultures is healing. Because sickness is thought of as a loss of the soul, the shaman must determine first whether the soul of the sick individual has strayed from the body or has been stolen by demons and is imprisoned in the other world. In the former case, the shaman captures the soul and reintegrates it in the body of the sick person. The latter case necessitates a descent to the netherworld, and this is a complicated and dangerous enterprise. Equally stirring is the voyage of the shaman to the other world to escort the soul of the deceased to its new abode. The shaman narrates to those present all the vicissitudes of the voyage as it goes on.

The "flight" of the shaman to heaven during initiation or ritual sacrifice can be regarded as the most ancient expression of mystical experience known to humankind. But the shaman is not only a mystic. He is just as much the guardian (and largely the creator) of the traditional lore of the tribe. The narrations of his adventurous descents to the netherworld and of his ascents to heaven constitute the material of popular epic poetry among many groups.

Two important concepts of the Innu and other Algonquian groups were manitou and the "big man" (a concept quite different from the "big men" of Melanesian cultures, who are local leaders). Manitou represents a pervasive power in the world that individuals can learn to use on their own behalf. The term Great Manitou, designating a personal god, probably represents a missionary-inspired adaptation of an older idea. A person's big man is an intimate spirit-being who confers wisdom, competence, skill, and strength in the food quest as well as in other areas of life, including magic. Maintaining a relationship with this being requires ethically good conduct. Animal-spirit "bosses" who control the supply of caribou, fish, and other creatures are another traditional belief shared by Algonquian and certain Athabaskan groups.

Three of the most popular characters in Algonquian folklore are Wiitiko (Windigo), a terrifying cannibalistic giant apt to be encountered in the forest; Tcikapis, a kindly, powerful young hero and the subject of many myths; and Wiskijan (Whiskeyjack), an amusing trickster. "Wiitiko psychosis" refers to a condition in which an individual would be seized by the obsessive idea that he was turning into a cannibal with a compulsive craving for human flesh.

Shamanism was an important feature of traditional Subarctic culture. The shaman, who could be male or female, served as a specialist curer and diviner in addition to his or her routine adult responsibilities. It was thought that occasionally shamans became evil and behaved malignantly. Shamanistic ability came to an individual from dreaming of animals who taught the dreamer to work with their aid. Such ability had to be validated through successful performance.

The Deg Xinag conceived of humans as comprising body, soul, and "speech," the latter an element surviving after death but, unlike the soul, not reincarnated. Hazards to life came from the soul always being menaced by various supernatural figures that were the primary enemies of human survival and by the souls of powerful evil shamans acting on behalf of these supernatural figures. In contrast, spirit-beings associated with animals and berries supported human survival. Animal songs and amulets created good relations with helpful animal spirits. Elaborate ceremonies in the men's house, to which the spirit-beings were invited, protected the food supply.

CULTURAL STABILITY AND ADJUSTMENT

Canadian and U.S. control over the American Subarctic peoples had been established by the late 19th century. The two countries supported the concept of assimilation for Indians (unlike other European colonial powers, which frequently advanced racial segregation), but their policy endeavoured to substitute indigenous ways of life with their own. Both countries used mechanisms such as compulsory education at boarding schools and the elimination of separate legal status for aboriginal peoples to implement their assimilationist goals.

During the 20th century, Subarctic peoples encountered profound local economic changes in addition to assimilationist policies. Well into the first third of the century, the northern subsistence economy continued to depend heavily upon hunting, while the cash economy derived almost entirely from the fur trade. During the Great Depression of the 1930s, demand for pelts drastically decreased, decimating the region's cash economy. Following World War II, new governmental restrictions on subsistence hunting and on trapping slowed economic recovery. In response to the increasing need for wage-based income, some indigenous families relocated from the forests and trading centres to established northern cities such as Fairbanks (Alaska), Whitehorse (Yukon), and Churchill (Manitoba), as well as to new towns, such as Schefferville (Quebec), Yellowknife (Northwest Territories), and Inuvik (Northwest Territories). These towns offered employment in industries such as commercial fishing, construction, mining, and defense. Expanding economic opportunities in the north also drew families from southern Canada, and for the first time fairly large numbers of indigenous Subarctic peoples and Euro-Americans interacted.

By the close of the 20th century, many Subarctic peoples had become involved in cultural preservation or revitalization movements, and a portion of those chose to

As the need for a wage-based income increased, many Subarctic families relocated to cities where employment such as mining was available. Joel Sartore/National Geographic Image Collection/Getty Images

remain in or relocate to smaller trading-post settlements to foster a more traditional lifestyle. Whether in rural or urban areas, many First Nations peoples and Native Alaskans began to view an intact forest landscape as an intrinsic part of their heritage. They became increasingly concerned about the economic development of the north and used a variety of means, from protest through land claims and other legal actions, to prevent or ameliorate the effects of such development. Many of their efforts have proven successful, most notably those resulting in the Alaskan Native Claim Settlement Act (U.S., 1971) and associated legislation and the creation of Nunavut (Canada, 1999), a province with a predominantly aboriginal government.

Chapter 4

SELECTED AMERICAN SUBARCTIC PEOPLES IN FOCUS

The Subarctic climate is dominated by the winter season, a long, bitterly cold period with short, clear days, relatively little precipitation (mostly in the form of snow), and low humidity. Its ecosystem was eminently suited to the production of fur-bearing animals. The following chapter treats two Subarctic groups who adapted to this climate and land.

EASTERN SUBARCTIC ZONE: ALGONQUIAN-LANGUAGE SPEAKERS

Of the two zones into which the Subarctic is commonly divided, the Eastern Subarctic is home to the Cree, the Innu (formerly Montagnais and Naskapi) of northern Quebec, and several groups of Ojibwa who, encouraged by the fur trade, displaced the Cree from what are now west-central Ontario and eastern Manitoba.

CREE

The Cree constitute a significant Algonquian-speaking group of North American Indians. Their realm incorporated a vast area from east of Hudson Bay and James Bay to as far west as Alberta and the Great Slave Lake in present-day Canada. Initially living in a smaller centre of this area, they expanded rapidly in the 17th and 18th centuries after engaging in the fur trade and acquiring firearms. The name Cree is a truncated form of Kristineaux, a French adaptation of the self-name of the James Bay band. Wars with the

A Cree hunter. Sam Abell/National Geographic Image Collection/
Getty Images

Dakota Sioux and Blackfoot and severe smallpox epidemics, notably in 1784 and 1838, reduced their numbers.

At the time of Canada's colonization by the French and English, there were two major divisions of Cree. Both were typical American Subarctic peoples. Traditionally, the Woodland Cree, also called Swampy Cree or Maskegon, subsisted by means of hunting, fowling, fishing, and collecting wild plant foods. They preferred hunting larger game such as caribou, moose, bear, and beaver but relied chiefly on hare for subsistence because of the scarcity of the other animals. The periodic scarcity of hare, however, sometimes caused famine. Woodland Cree social organization was based on bands of related families, with large groups coalescing for warfare. Fears of witchcraft and a respect for a variety of taboos and customs relating to the spirits of game animals pervaded historical Cree culture. Shamans wielded great power.

The Plains Cree lived on the northern Great Plains. Like other Plains Indians, their traditional economy focused on bison hunting and gathering wild plant foods. After acquiring horses and firearms, they were more militant than the Woodland Cree, raiding and warring against other Plains tribes. Reportedly divided into 12 independent bands, each with its own chief, the Plains Cree also had a military system that integrated and organized warriors from all the bands. Religion and ceremony were highly valued as means of fostering success in war and the bison hunt. The Assiniboin were the traditional allies of both the Plains and the Woodland Cree.

Early 21st-century population estimates indicated some 90,000 individuals of Cree descent.

INNU

The Innu are an amalgamation of two groups, also called Montagnais and Naskapi. Although their Algonquian dialects were practically identical, their material cultures diverged. This was evident particularly in their acclimatization to their particular surroundings. The southern Innu, or Montagnais, traditionally occupied a large forested area paralleling the northern shores of the Gulf of St. Lawrence, lived in birchbark wickiups, or wigwams, and subsisted on moose, salmon, eel, and seal. The northern Innu, or Naskapi, lived on the vast Labrador plateau of grasslands and tundra, hunted caribou for both food and skins to cover their wickiups, and supplemented their diet with fish and small game. The name Montagnais is French, meaning "mountaineers." Naskapi is an indigenous name thought to mean "rude, uncivilized people," an apparent reference to their remote frontier life. The Naskapi called themselves Nenenot, meaning "true, real people." In the late 20th century, the two closely related groups jointly adopted the name Innu ("people").

Innu people living to the south dressed in robes, loincloths or dresses, leggings, and moccasins, much like their southern neighbours—and ancient enemies—the

Northern Innu clothing, like this Naskapi coat, closely resembled that of the coastal Eskimo. SuperStock/Getty Images

Iroquois and Mi'kmaq. More northerly Innu people wore tailored clothing similar to that of the coastal Eskimo, their only traditional foes. For both groups canoes furnished transportation in summer. Snowshoes and dogsleds were used in winter. Religious belief involved animism and centred on manitou, or supernatural power, with much importance also attached to various nature and animal spirits, both evil and benevolent.

Innu people avoided the creation of formal political structures. Tribal organization comprised small bands of related families that often shifted in composition as individual leaders rose and fell. After the European colonization of the Americas began, the southern bands formalized their trapping and hunting territories somewhat to better engage in the fur trade. The northern territories were larger and more loosely defined.

Population estimates indicated some 9,500 Innu descendants in the early 21st century.

OJIBWA

The Ojibwa (also spelled Ojibwe or Ojibway, also called Chippewa) are an Algonquian-speaking tribe. Anishinaabe, their name for themselves, means "original people." At one time the Ojibwa inhabited present-day Ontario and Manitoba, Can., and Minnesota and North Dakota, U.S., from Lake Huron westward onto the Plains. In Canada those Ojibwa who lived west of Lake Winnipeg are called the Saulteaux. When first reported in the *Relations* of 1640, an annual report by the Jesuit missionaries in New France, the Ojibwa occupied a comparatively restricted region near the St. Mary's River and in the Upper Peninsula of the present state of Michigan. They moved west as the fur trade expanded, in response to pressure from tribes to their east and new opportunities to their west.

Traditionally, each Ojibwa tribe was divided into migratory bands. In the autumn, bands separated into family units, which dispersed to individual hunting areas. In summer, families gathered together, usually at fishing sites. The Ojibwa relied on the collection of wild rice for a major part of their diet, and a few bands also cultivated corn (maize). Birch bark was used extensively for canoes, dome-shaped wickiups, and utensils. Clan intermarriage served to connect a people that otherwise avoided overall tribal or national chiefs. Chieftainship of a band was not a powerful office until dealings with fur traders strengthened the position, which then became hereditary through the paternal line. The annual celebration hosted by the Midewiwin (Grand Medicine Society), a secret religious organization

MIDEWIWIN

The Grand Medicine Society of the Ojibwa peoples of North America is called Midewiwin. According to Ojibwa religion, assorted supernatural beings initially carried out Midewiwin rituals to soothe Minabozho—a culture hero and negotiator between the Great Spirit and humans—when his brother died. Minabozho, having pity on the suffering inherent in the human condition, transmitted the ritual to the spirit-being Otter and, through Otter, to the Ojibwa.

Traditionally, the Grand Medicine Society was an esoteric group consisting at times of more than 1,000 members, including shamans, prophets, and seers, as well as others who successfully undertook the initiation process. The society was thus both a centre of spiritual knowledge and a source of social prestige.

With a complex series of four degrees of initiation that were held within an especially constructed medicine lodge, the society's central acts involved the ritual death and rebirth of the initiate. The powers of an initiate included not only those of healing and causing death but also those of obtaining food for the tribe and victory in battle.

open to men and women, was the major Ojibwa ceremonial. Membership was believed to provide supernatural assistance and conferred prestige on its members.

The Ojibwa constituted one of the largest indigenous North American groups in the early 21st century, when population estimates indicated some 175,000 individuals of Ojibwa descent.

WESTERN SUBARCTIC ZONE: ATHABASKAN-LANGUAGE SPEAKERS

The Western zone extends from Canada into Alaska. Because it is composed of two distinct cultures, this zone is often further subdivided into a region drained mostly by the northward-flowing Mackenzie River system and home to the mobile and less socially stratified Chipewyan, Beaver, Slave, and Kaska nations, and a region notable for salmon streams that drain into the Pacific Ocean. The inhabitants of the latter area include the Carrier, part of the Gwich'in, the Tanaina, and the Deg Xinag.

BEAVER

The Beaver people (self-name Dane-zaa, Dunnezaa) derive their name from the Indian word for their main site, Tsades, or River of Beavers (presently known as the Peace River). The small band lives in the mountainous riverine areas of northwestern Alberta and northeastern British Columbia, Canada. They were forced westward into that area in the early 18th century as the well-armed Cree, who were deeply involved in the European fur trade.

Traditionally, the Beaver were scattered in independent nomadic bands, each with its own hunting territory. They hunted moose, caribou, bears, and bison. They were led by shamans called "dreamers." The Beaver lived in

skin-covered tepees in winter and brush-covered tepees
or lean-tos in summer, and they traveled mainly by canoe.
At least, that is how they lived when first encountered
by Europeans, after they had adopted many cultural
elements of the Cree. At the end of the 20th century,
researchers determined that the Beaver had made use of
a different type of dwelling prior to their contact with the
Cree. Earlier they had lived in shelters divided into two
rooms—one for storage and the other for sleeping—by a
passageway having an entrance or exit at either end.

In the 21st century they occupied four reservations,
including the region of Horse Lake near Hythe, Alta.; on
the upper Halfway River northwest of Fort St. John, B.C.;
on the Blueberry River north of Fort St. John; and on the
Doig River just east of the Halfway River reserve. As sign-
ers of Treaty 8 (1899), the Beaver have the right to hunt,
trap, and fish throughout their territory. Beaver descendants numbered more than 750 in the early 21st century.

CARRIER

The Carrier name ("Porteur" in French) originated with
the custom of widows carrying their departed hus-
bands' ashes in knapsacks for three years. The name
Takulli ("People Who Go upon the Water") by which
they are also known, may be a misunderstanding of
their self-name, Dakelh. The Carrier are centred in the
upper branches of the Fraser River between the Coast
Mountains and the Rocky Mountains in what is now
central British Columbia. Although their original territory was significantly inland from the Pacific, traditional
Carrier culture shared a number of the customs of the
Northwest Coast Indians.

The Carrier were semisedentary, moving seasonally
between villages and hunting and fishing camps. Southern

Carrier people lived in semisubterranean houses. Northern Carrier people made gabled houses of poles and planks, much like those of their coastal neighbours. Both types of dwellings were communal.

Carrier social organization was also much like that of the coastal tribes, though without the slavery commonly practiced among those neighbours. It included elaborate class structures composed of nobles and commoners, usually with complex obligations to marry outside one's lineage, clan, and house. Each subgroup had exclusive rights to its territory, and encroachments by other subgroups constituted grounds for reprisal or compensation. The Carrier practiced the potlatch, the custom of large gift-giving feasts or ceremonies for the recognition of such significant events as marriage.

Carrier economics relied chiefly on the plentiful river salmon, which the people supplemented by hunting various kinds of local game and collecting wild plant foods. They exploited resources from the abundant woodlands and had a woodworking tradition that created highly decorated utilitarian items such as canoes, weapons, and cooking vessels. Carrier craftsmen carved pillars, commonly referred to as totem poles, depicting the crests of noble-status individuals and lineages, as well as spirit-beings from religion, myth, and legend. Carrier religious beliefs centred on a great sky god and numerous spirits in nature which were contacted through dreams, visions, ritual, and magic. They also believed in both reincarnation and an afterlife.

Early 21st-century population estimates indicated more than 1,000 Carrier descendants.

CHIPEWYAN

Northern Canada's Chipewyan people first lived in boreal forests separated by stretches of barren ground. Their settlement was an ample triangular region. Its base ran along the 1,000-mile-long (1,600 km) Churchill River with the tip some 700 miles (1,100 km) to the north.

Traditionally organized into many independent bands, the Chipewyan were nomads following the seasonal movement of the caribou. These animals were their chief source of food and of skins for clothing, tents, nets, and lines, although the Chipewyan also relied upon bison, musk oxen, moose, waterfowl, fish, and wild plants for subsistence.

When the Hudson's Bay Company established a fur-trading post at the mouth of the Churchill River in 1717, the Chipewyan intensified their hunting of fur animals. Members of the tribe also took advantage of their geographic location between the British traders and tribes farther inland, acting as middlemen in the fur exchange by brokering deals with the Yellowknife and Dogrib tribes farther west. Until new trading posts were established in western North America, Chipewyan individuals were able to exact huge profits from this trade. A smallpox epidemic in 1781 decimated the Chipewyan, and subsequent periods of disease and malnutrition further reduced their numbers.

Historically, Chipewyan culture was depicted as rather ruthless. By the mid-20th century such characterizations were generally thought to be inaccurate. Early 21st-century anthropologists characterized traditional Chipewyan culture as one in which individuals typically preferred subtlety to overt action. These anthropologists also described social and individual flexibility (rather than ruthlessness) as important strategies used by the Chipewyan for coping with their difficult northern environment.

Population estimates in the early 21st century indicated more than 1,500 Chipewyan descendants.

DEG XINAG

The Deg Xinag (also called Deg Hit'an) inhabit interior Alaska, chiefly the basins of the upper Kuskokwim and lower Yukon rivers. (The name Ingalik, by which they were formerly known, is considered perjorative.) Their region is mountainous, with both woodlands and tundra, and is fairly rich in fish, caribou, bear, moose, and other game on which the Deg Xinag traditionally subsisted—fish, fresh or dried, being central to their diet. Before colonization, Deg Xinag and Eskimo (Inuit) technology were somewhat similar: the Deg Xinag wore parkas and trousers, built semisubterranean sod houses, and used harpoons, spear-throwers, and weapons similar to those of the Eskimo. However, in most ways the traditional Deg Xinag were more similar to other American Subarctic peoples than to their Arctic neighbours.

Traditionally, the Deg Xinag lived in villages. Permanent winter settlements for a fairly large group were complemented by seasonal fishing and hunting camps that sheltered a few families each. The centre of village life was a large semisubterranean lodge called a *kashim*. The *kashim* served several functions, mostly for men, providing a venue for sweat baths, council meetings, entertainment, funerals, and shamanic rituals. Women's activities tended to take place in family dwellings and in the open air. Deg Xinag people were much given to games and sports, ceremonies, and potlatches. The latter are gift-giving festivities through which the sponsors acquire prestige. Potlatches frequently mark life passages such as marriage and death.

Although traditional Deg Xinag religion included a creator, a devil, and other worlds beyond the living, it was more concerned with a kind of supernatural spirit that

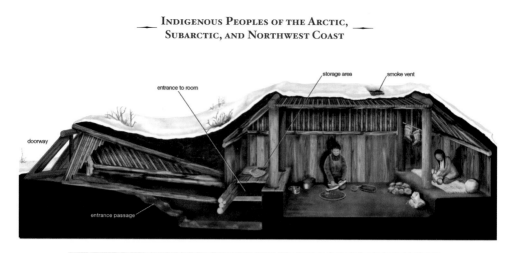

Cross-section of a traditional semisubterranean dwelling of the North American Arctic and Subarctic peoples. © Encyclopædia Britannica, Inc.; adapted using information from The Field Museum, Chicago

pervaded all things animate and inanimate in the world. There were several ceremonies, taboos, and superstitions relating to animals and the hunt and to the care of tools and other economic items. As with other societies that practiced animism, the Deg Xinag believed that survival and success required good relations with the things of nature.

Early 21st-century population estimates indicated some 150 individuals of Deg Xinag descent.

DOGRIB

The Dogrib, who call themselves Thlingchadinne, Tlicho, or Doné, live in the forested and barren-ground areas between the Great Bear and Great Slave lakes in the Northwest Territories, Canada. There are six settlements: Behchoko (formerly Rae-Edzo), Whati (Lac la Martre), Gameti, Wekweeti (Snare Lake), Detah, and N'dilo (a subcommunity of Yellowknife). The name Dogrib is an English adaptation of their own name, Thlingchadinne, or

Dog-Flank People, referring to their fabled descent from a supernatural dog-man.

Traditionally, the Dogrib fished and hunted, subsisting chiefly on barren-ground caribou, which were trapped or speared. Moose, hare, fish, and migratory water birds were also important foods. The usual habitation of the Dogrib was a skin-covered tent, although in the hard winters they sometimes built wooden and brush-covered lodges. Their social organization consisted of many independent loosely led bands, each with its own territory. The chief enemies of the Dogrib were the Cree, Chipewyan, and Yellowknife. The Dogrib eventually massacred many Yellowknife in raids in the late 18th and early 19th centuries. Since that time the leaders of both groups have declared peace.

The Dogrib remained relatively isolated until the mid-20th century, when improved transportation and communication facilities brought them into greater contact with other parts of Canada. Dogrib descendants numbered more than 3,000 in the early 21st century.

Gwich'in

The Gwich'in (or Kutchin) peoples live in the Yukon River and Peel River basins of eastern Alaska and Yukon. This area is made up of coniferous forests mixed with sweeping, desolate land. The name Gwich'in means "people" and refers collectively to an indefinite number of distinct American Subarctic peoples, there being no precise agreement among authorities on whom to include under this cover name, which is as much linguistic as cultural.

In traditional Gwich'in social organization, men became chiefs by demonstrating leadership or prowess in hunting or war. Men's major pursuits included battle, fishing, and hunting caribou, moose, and other game.

Women's pursuits included making nearly all household goods, gathering wild plant foods, and transporting their families and material possessions during frequent moves from one camp to another.

The Gwich'in people's most influential neighbours were the Eskimo, or Inuit, with whom they traded and fought and from whom they borrowed such cultural traits as tailored caribou-skin clothing (most conspicuously, the Eskimo hood and mittens), various hunting weapons, and the sled. They also shared customs with tribes to the south and east—painting their faces and hair, wearing feathers as hair ornaments, and decorating their clothing with fringes and beads. Gwich'in houses were domed structures of poles and fir boughs, banked with snow in winter and ventilated by a smoke hole at the top. Little is known of Gwich'in religion or beliefs, but they were well known for their feasts, games (especially wrestling), singing, and dancing.

Early 21st-century population estimates indicated more than 4,500 individuals of Gwich'in descent.

Kaska

The Kaska are a group of First Nations (Indian) peoples living in the forested mountains between the two great ranges, the Coast Mountains and the Rocky Mountains, in northeastern British Columbia and southeastern Yukon. The nomadic Kaska were primarily caribou hunters and lived in temporary dwellings—tepees or huts made of poles and brush or, sometimes in summer, simple lean-tos. Transport was by canoe, snowshoe, and toboggan. Although not much is known of their religious beliefs (or of their customs), apparently they, like the Sekani farther south, believed in animal spirits and in the practices of medicine men. Their language is mutually intelligible with that of the Tahltan and Tagish.

The Kaska continued to inhabit their traditional lands, and in the early 21st century the Kaska in British Columbia were negotiating a treaty settlement. Although they considered themselves one nation, the Kaska were divided by the Indian Act into five bands, now considered First Nations. The B.C. groups were the Dease River First Nation at Good Hope Lake; Daylu Dena Council at Lower Post; and the Kwadacha First Nation at Fort Ware, north of Prince George. The Yukon groups were the Liard First Nation at Watson Lake and the Ross River Dena Council at Ross River. Early 21st-century population estimates indicated some 2,200 Kaska descendants.

SEKANI

The Sekani (also spelled Tsek'ehne) lived mostly in river valleys on the eastern and western slopes of the Rocky Mountains in what are now British Columbia and Alberta, Can. They were often harassed by the neighbouring Cree, Beaver, Carrier, and Shuswap peoples and, during the British colonization of Canada, by fur trappers and miners. Disease and malnutrition resulting from the depletion of game compounded Sekani hardships during this period.

Traditionally a nomadic hunting and gathering culture, the Sekani were divided into several loosely organized independent bands with fluid leadership. The name Sekani, meaning "dwellers on the rocks," originally denoted only one particular band. Homes were casually built huts or lean-tos, each framed by poles and covered with spruce bark or brush. For food the Sekani preferred moose, caribou, bears, mountain goats, beavers, and other game, which they hunted with snares, bows and arrows, spears, and clubs. They scorned fish, avoiding it unless facing dire food shortages and deriding the neighbouring Carrier as "fish eaters."

Sekani religious beliefs involved animism, the tenet that spirits or powers exist throughout the natural world among animals, plants, landforms, and weather events such as thunder. Each male had one or more guardian spirits associated with birds or other animals from which he might elicit power on occasions of great need. Shamans were considered able to cause and cure illness.

Early 21st-century population estimates indicated some 1,200 Sekani descendants.

SLAVE

Canada's Slave people first populated the Great Slave Lake's western coasts, the Mackenzie River and Liard River basins, and other adjacent riverine and forest areas. The Cree, who looted their property and enslaved many of them, called them Awokanak, or Slave. This was the name by which they became known, even to the French and English. Whether or not it was deserved, the Slave had a general reputation for timidity or pacifism.

Like most other Athabaskan tribes, the Slave were separated into a number of independent bands, each of which was rather loosely organized, with only nominal leaders, and was associated with certain hunting territories. An informal council of hunters settled disputes. Women and the aged were treated with a respect and kindness that was not typical of all Athabaskans.

The Slave were inhabitants of the forests and riverbanks. They hunted moose, woodland caribou, and other game but also relied heavily on fish for food. Animal skins were made into robes, shirts, leggings, moccasins, and other clothing. Fringes and ornaments made of antlers, porcupine quills, and other natural materials were popular. Their dwellings consisted of brush-covered tepees in

Slave women and the aged were regarded with respect, which was unusual among other Athabaskans. Raymond Gehman/National Geographic Image Collection/Getty Images

summer and rectangular huts formed of poles and spruce branches in winter.

The Slave believed in guardian spirits, in the power of medicine men, and in an undefined life after death. A common practice was the deathbed confession of sins, thought to contribute to the delay of death.

Early 21st-century population estimates indicated some 7,000 Slave descendants.

TAHLTAN

The Tahltan lived on the upper Stikine River and other nearby streams in present-day northwestern British Columbia, Can. This region, though grassy and rocky with only sparse woodlands, provided plentiful salmon and such game as caribou, moose, bears, and various other fur-bearing animals.

Traditionally the Tahltan were nomadic, gathering at salmon runs in summer and dispersing to hunting territories in winter. Tahltan society was organized through kinship. There were six clans headed by chiefs and grouped three and three into the Raven and the Wolf subgroups, or moieties. The moieties had reciprocal ceremonial functions, reciprocal marital obligations (a Raven person had to marry a Wolf person and vice versa), and ownership of separate hunting grounds, though in practice the latter division was often ignored. In the 18th century, the Wolf group added a fourth clan, making seven clans altogether. This form of organization was similar to that of other Northwest Coast Indians, as was Tahltan social stratification, which included classes of nobles, commoners, and

The Stikine River Valley in British Columbia, Canada. This region was home to the Tahltan. Sarah Leen/National Geographic Image Collection/Getty Images

slaves. Tahltan dwellings were made of poles, bark, and brush, and a typical central village included a more substantial 100-foot (30-m) ceremonial and residential lodge for the chiefly families of the clans.

Tahltan individuals and families sponsored the potlatch, a gift-giving festival held for validating ennoblement, advancing one's prestige, or marking an event, such as a funeral. They also carried on trade, as well as some raiding and warfare, with the coastal tribes and with the Kaska to the north.

The Tahltan recognized a sun god and a sky god. However, their religion was more focused on animism, a belief in the supernatural powers of the natural world, particularly of the creatures that constituted their food supply. The spirits seen in dreams or visions and evoked by medicine men were almost invariably animals.

Early 21st-century population estimates indicated some 3,000 individuals of Tahltan descent.

TANAINA

Other than the Tanaina peoples, no other northern Athabaskan-speaking group inhabited widespread areas of the ocean's coast. They made their homes in the drainage regions of Cook Inlet and Clark Lake in present-day southern Alaska. They called themselves Tanaina, meaning "the people." They have also been called Knaiakhotana ("people of the Kenai Peninsula").

Like the Northwest Coast Indians, the Tanaina traditionally subsisted mainly on salmon and other fish (as well as shellfish). They also hunted bears, mountain sheep and goats, moose, caribou, and other game for both skins and food. Their dwellings consisted of semisubterranean log-and-sod houses for winter use and a variety of casually built shelters for summer use during the salmon runs. The latter also served as smokehouses for drying the fish catch. For transportation they used the skin-covered kayak and the open umiak, as well as snowshoes and sleds.

Tanaina society was organized on the basis of kinship and class. Each individual belonged to a clan. Membership in a clan was traced through the female line. The clans were grouped into two large phratries (kinship groups), one comprising five clans and the other six clans. Marriages always drew one partner from each phratry. There were also two social classes—nobles and commoners—and each village usually had a chief of sorts. More-organized leadership, with clear leaders and councils, usually developed only for warfare and raiding (their chief foes being the Eskimo or Inuit).

Tanaina individuals and families used the potlatch to increase their prestige through the ostentatious giving of gifts. Animism was at the core of Tanaina religion. They believed that all things in nature were suffused with supernatural powers and that guardian spirits shadowed everyone. Taboos, tokens, and amulets were numerous. Shamanism was also quite influential. Some shamans were chiefs.

Early 21st-century population estimates indicated some 100 individuals of Tanaina descent.

Of the several culture areas of native North America, the Northwest Coast was the most sharply delineated, thanks to ocean and landforms. Stretching from Yakutat Bay in the northeastern Gulf of Alaska south to Cape Mendocino in present-day California, it also included offshore islands. To the east it extended the crest of the Coast Ranges and the Cascades south to parts of what is now Oregon and northwestern California. Despite the region's distinct physical boundaries, the transition from the Northwest Coast to the California culture area is gradual, and some scholars classify the southernmost tribes discussed in this section as California Indians.

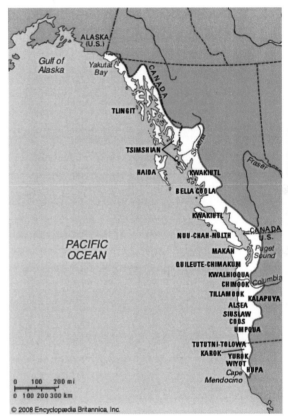

Distribution of Northwest Coast Indians. Copyright Encyclopædia Britannica, Inc.; rendering for this edition by Rosen Educational Services

The Kuroshio, a Pacific Ocean current, warms the region. Temperatures are rarely hot and seldom drop below freezing. The offshore current also deluges the region with rain. Although it falls rather unevenly across the region, annual precipitation averages more than 160 inches (406 cm) in some areas and rarely drops below 30 inches (76 cm) in even the driest climatic zones. The northern Coast Range averages an elevation of about 3,300 feet (1,000 metres) above sea level, with some peaks and ridges rising to more than 6,600 feet (2,000 metres). In most of the Northwest, the land rises steeply from the sea and is cut by a myriad of narrow channels and fjords. The shores of Puget Sound, southwestern Washington, and the Oregon coast hills are lower and less rugged.

In general, traditional Northwest Coast economies were oriented toward aquatic resources. The region's coastal forests—dense and predominantly coniferous, with spruces, Douglas fir, hemlock, red and yellow cedar, and, in the south, coast redwood—supported abundant fauna and a wide variety of wild plant foods.

ORGANIZATION OF LANGUAGE AND TERRITORY

The languages of the Northwest Coast were many and diverse. Starting in the north, the divisions include Tlingit, Haida, Tsimshian, northern Kwakiutl, Bella Coola (Nuxalk), southern Kwakiutl, Nuu-chah-nulth (Nootka), Coast Salish, Quileute-Chimakum, Kwalhioqua, and Chinook. Among the peoples living along the Oregon coast and in northwestern California, a smaller group of languages were spoken, including Tillamook, Alsea, Siuslaw, Umpqua, Coos, Tututni-Tolowa, Yurok, Wiyot, and Hupa.

Northwest Coast groups can be classified into four units or "provinces." The northern province included speakers of Tlingit, Haida, Tsimshian, and the Tsimshian-influenced

Haisla (northernmost Heiltsuq or Kwakiutl). The Wakashan province included all other Kwakiutl, the Bella Coola, and the Nuu-chah-nulth. The Coast Salish–Chinook province extended south to the central coast of Oregon and included the Makah, Chinook, Tillamook, Siuslaw, and others. The northwestern California province included the Athabaskan-speaking Tututni-Tolowa as well as the Karok, Yurok, Wiyot, and Hupa.

The Northwest Coast was densely populated when Europeans first made landfall in the 18th century. Estimates of density in terms of persons per square mile mean little in a region where long stretches of coast consist of uninhabitable cliffs rising from the sea. However, early historic sources indicate that many winter villages had hundreds of inhabitants.

CLASS STRUCTURE AND COMMUNITY ORGANIZATION

As a rule, hunting and gathering cultures are portrayed as using uncomplicated tools, having few belongings, and being minimal egalitarian groups. The groups of the Northwest Coast (in this instance fishing and gathering peoples, rather than hunting and gathering) are a conspicuous exception to this rule. Because food abounded in this region, less work was required to meet the subsistence needs of the population than in farming societies of comparable size. And, as with agricultural societies, the food surpluses of the Northwest encouraged the development of social stratification. The region's traditional cultures typically had a ruling elite that controlled use rights to corporately held or communal property, with a "house society" form of social organization. The best analogues for such cultures are generally agreed to be the medieval societies of Europe, China, and Japan, with their so-called noble houses.

In house societies the key social and productive unit was a flexible group of a few dozen to 100 or more people who considered themselves to be related (sometimes only distantly), who were coresident in houses or estates for at least part of the year, and who held common title to important resources. In the Northwest those resources included sites for fishing, berry picking, hunting, and habitation. House groups also held a variety of less tangible privileges, including the exclusive use of particular names, songs, dances, and, especially in the north, totemic representations or crests.

Within a house group, each member had a social rank that was valued according to the individual's degree of relatedness to a founding ancestor. Although social stratification in Northwest Coast communities is frequently described as including three divisions—chiefly elites, commoners, and slaves or war captives—each person in fact had a particular hereditary status that placed him within the group as though he occupied one step on a long staircase of statuses, with the eldest of the senior line on the highest step and the most remotely related at the bottom. Strictly speaking, each person was in a class by himself.

The highest in rank invariably held a special title that in each language was translated into English as "chief." This person administered the group's properties. Usually a man or the widow of a past chief, this leader made decisions regarding the patterns of daily life—when to move to the salmon-fishing station, when to build weirs and traps, when to make the first catch, when and where to perform the rite propitiating the first salmon of the season, which other groups should be invited to feasts, and so on. A chief had many prerogatives and sumptuary privileges and in turn was expected to administer efficiently and tend to the social and ritual affairs that ensured the general welfare and prestige of the group.

Notionally, those of high rank had vast authoritarian powers. However, within the group all mature persons other than slaves could voice their opinions on group affairs, for a house group's property was held in common. Most leaders refrained from abusing other members of the house and community—not only were they kin, but the chief also needed their cooperation to accomplish even the most basic tasks. For example, multiple strong arms and sturdy backs were needed to obtain, assemble, and position the heavy materials required to build or repair a house, to construct fish weirs and traps, and to launch and paddle the chief's huge dugout canoe. Singers, dancers, and attendants were necessary to stage important cere-monies properly, and bold warriors were needed to defend the group against foes. Leaders were also aware that there was enough flexibility in the social structure that those of low rank could abandon an abusive situation and move in with kindred elsewhere.

Slaves, however, had few or no rights of participation in house group decisions. They usually had been captured in childhood and taken or traded so far from their original homes that they had little hope of finding their way back. They were chattels who might be treated well or ill, traded off, slain, married, or freed at their owner's whim. A typi-cal house group owned at least one slave but rarely more than a dozen. Their duties generally included boring, rep-etitious, and messy work such as stocking the house with firewood and water. In some groups, slaves could achieve better social standing by displaying an unusual talent, such as luck in gambling, which made them eligible for mar-riage to a person of higher status.

Insignia or other devices often were used to signal per-sonal status. Chiefly people often wore robes of sea otter fur, as otter pelts were quite valuable in the fur trade. The quality and level of decoration on clothing marked other statuses as well. Head flattening was considered a beautifying process from the northern Kwakiutl region to the central Oregon coast, as well as among some of the neighbouring Plateau Indians. This painless, gradual procedure involved binding a newborn child's head to a cradle board in such a way as to produce a long subconical form, a strong slope from the eyebrows back, or a distinctive wedge shape in which the back of the skull was flattened. In the Northwest Coast culture area, head flattening was practiced only on relatively high-status infants, although the capture and enslavement of children from neighbouring tribes that also undertook this modification meant that a shapely head was no guarantee of an individual's current status.

The status of each member of a house group was hereditary but was not automatically assumed at birth. Such things had to be formally and publicly announced at a potlatch, an event sponsored by each group north of the Columbia River. The term comes from the trade jargon used throughout the region and means "to give." A potlatch always involved the invitation of another house (or houses), whose members were received with great formality as guests and witnesses of the event. Potlatches were used to mark a wide variety of transitions, including marriages, the building of a house, chiefly funerals, and the bestowal of adult names, noble titles, crests, and ceremonial rights.

Having witnessed the proceedings, the guests were given gifts and served prodigious amounts of food with the expectation that what was left uneaten would be taken home. The social statuses of the guests were recognized and reified through the potlatch, for gifts were distributed in rank order and the more splendid gifts were given to the guests of highest status. Whether hosting or acting as guests at a potlatch, all members of a house usually participated in the proceedings, a process that served to strengthen their identification with the group.

The potlatch was part of a formal ceremony that marked a number of important events, including marriages, births, and deaths. Apic/Hulton Archive/Getty Images

Although potlatches shared some fundamental characteristics across cultures, there were also regional variations. In the northern province, for example, a major potlatch was part of the cycle of mortuary observances after the death of a chief, at which his heir formally assumed chiefly status. In the Wakashan and Salish regions, a chief gave a potlatch before his own demise in order to bestow office on his successor.

Some early anthropologists argued that the potlatch was an economic enterprise in which the giver expected to recover a profit on the goods he had distributed when, in turn, his guests became potlatch hosts. However, this was an impossibility because only a few guests of highest rank would ever stage such affairs and invite their former hosts. Those of intermediate and low rank could not afford to do so, yet the value of the gifts bestowed on them was considerable. Indeed, before the fur trade made great quantities of manufactured goods available, potlatches were few, whereas feasts, though also formal but not occasions for bestowing titles and gifts, were frequent occurrences.

SUBSISTENCE, TRANSPORT, AND SHELTER

Peoples of the Northwest Coast had an interrelated and complex economy. Perhaps the best example of this can be seen in their efficient management of natural resources. Aquatic resources were particularly abundant and included herring, oil-rich candlefish (eulachon), smelt, cod, halibut, mollusks, five species of salmon, and gray whales. However, the fisheries were scattered across the region and not equally easy to exploit. Certain species of salmon, for example, traveled upriver from the sea to spawn each year, but only in certain rivers and only at particular times of the year.

Generally, the important species for preservation for winter stores were the pink and the chum salmon. Because these species ceased to feed for some time before entering fresh water, their flesh had less fat and when smoked and dried would keep for a long period of time. Other salmon species, such as sockeye, coho, and the flavoursome chinook or king salmon, were eaten immediately or dried and kept for a short period, but their high fat content caused the meat to spoil relatively quickly even when dried. Therefore, the principal fishing sites were those along rivers and streams in which pink or chum salmon ran in the fall. In the spring other sorts of fish became available in tremendous schools: herring came in to spawn in coves, candlefish entered certain rivers, and, farther south, smelt spawned on sandy beaches in summer. People also went to sea to hunt marine mammals and to fish for offshore species such as halibut.

Water transport was highly important in the region for subsistence purposes and as a way to effect trade between tribes and later with fur traders. All groups made efficient dugout canoes. Northern groups, as well as the Kwakiutl and Salish down to Puget Sound, made dugouts with vertical cutwaters, or projecting bow and stern pieces, as well as those with rounded sterns and hulls. The Nuu-chah-nulth and some of their neighbours made vessels with curving cutwaters at the bow, vertical sterns, and angular flat bottoms. Northwestern California dugouts had upturned rounded ends, rounded hulls, carved seats, and foot braces for the steersman. Watercraft were made in different proportions for different purposes. For instance, large reinforced vessels were used to move people and cargo, while shorter, narrower craft were used for sea mammal hunting.

Summer was a time for hard work. Food had to be caught or gathered and processed for winter consumption. Usually homesites and settlements were limited to narrow beaches or terraces because the land fell so steeply to the shore or riverbank. Between the limited number of building sites and the uneven distribution of natural resources, it was most efficient for a house group to have several bases of operation. In summer they dispersed into small groups that moved among fishing and berry-picking sites and other established but minor residential areas as their resources became available.

Most people spent the winter in villages with several sizable houses (each with its associated group) as well as at least one sizable structure in which the highest-ranking group lived and where the village could hold a large potlatch. During winter people of higher status rarely worked at day-to-day activities (leaving that to slaves), instead using the time to create two- and three-dimensional art and conduct potlatches, dances, and sacred ceremonies that brought people together to socialize, trade, and negotiate relationships within and between communities. For instance, from Tlingit country in the north to at least as far south as Puget Sound and perhaps farther, several house groups would typically pass the winter together at a site in a sheltered cove that was protected from winter winds. During this period the relative prestige of each group and individual was factored into all interactions. These assemblages of multiple house groups at winter village sites are often called "tribes," but it must be noted that such units were not politically integrated, for each of the component houses retained its economic and political autonomy.

As structures, Northwest Coast houses shared a few significant traits. All were rectilinear in floor plan, with plank walls and a plank roof, and all but those of northwestern California were large. In the north, most houses were built on a nearly square plan, reaching sizes as large as 50 feet wide by 55 feet long (15.25 by 16.75 m). They were typically constructed around a deep central pit, with vertical plank walls and a gabled roof intermeshed for stability. To the south, in the Wakashan province, houses were typically rectangular and reached sizes of approximately 40 feet by 60 to 100 feet (12 metres by 18.25 to 30.5 m). Huge cedar posts with side beams and ridgepoles constituted a permanent framework to which were attached wall planks and roof planks that could be taken down, loaded onto canoes, and transported from one site to another.

Some peoples in the Coast Salish–Chinook province also built houses of permanent frameworks with detachable siding and roofing, although they generally used a shed roof system with one slope instead of a peaked roof. Along the lower Columbia River, the typical house was built over a large rectangular pit that was fairly deep and lined with planks, as the earth provided excellent insulation against the cold and damp. Only the gabled roof and its end supports showed above ground. At the southernmost limit of the culture area, the northwestern California house type was designed for single-family use. These homes were constructed over a central pit, with low side walls of redwood planks and a three-pitch roof somewhat reminiscent of a pyramid. The peoples of northwestern California also built a combined clubhouse and sweat house that was the focus of male activity. These multipurpose structures were common to many California Indian groups.

MATERIALS AND THE VISUAL ARTS

The densely forested milieu of the indigenous peoples of the Northwest Coast influenced both the technologies they embraced and the materials they used in artistic expression. Some species of trees were readily available and easily worked, such as giant arborvitae (*Thuja plicata*, or red cedar) and the redwood (*Sequoia sempervirens*). The trunks of these trees could be split into planks or hollowed out into canoes, containers, and other useful objects.

The peoples of this region were noted for their artistic skill, and everyday items usually were decorated in some way. More than most other groups in North America, Northwest Coast visual arts emphasized symmetry, neatness of finish, and embellishment through carving and painting. Traditional carving implements included adzes, mauls, wedges, chisels, drills, and curved knives, all made of stone. Sharkskin was used for sanding or polishing wooden items.

As far south as the Columbia River, wooden boxes were made of red cedar boards that were kerfed—cut nearly through transversely. The wood was steamed at these points until it was flexible enough to shape into the form of a box. Dishes often were hollowed out of pieces of wood, sometimes plain, sometimes in the form of animals or monsters. Other items made of wood included spoons and ladles, canoe bailers, trinket boxes, chamber pots, masks and rattles used in ceremonies, magnificent memorial or totem poles and interior house posts, housefronts and screens, halibut hooks, and even the triggers of animal traps. Sometimes items were made from the horns of mountain goats, bighorn sheep, or elk, which were carved by essentially the same methods as wood. Occasionally sculptures were carved from stone.

Artists in the northern province emphasized low-relief carving accented by painting. Their motifs were the hereditary crests of the clans or parts of the crests. Different groups in the northern province expressed themselves in somewhat different styles. Haida art, for instance, tended to be massive and to comprise highly conventionalized balanced elements. In Tsimshian carving and painting, there was an effort to leave no open space in or between the conventionalized motifs. Filler elements such as eye designs and miniature figures were used intensively. Tlingit art was slightly less conventionalized, with relatively little use of filler elements.

In the Wakashan province, representative art was frankly sculptural, impressionistic, and bold. There was a limited amount of simple geometric design on such things as whalebone clubs and whaling harpoon barbs. Their Coast Salish neighbours used some, but less, representative art, similar if looser in style. On Puget Sound there was little representative art. The abstract painted designs on the canoe boards were unlike anything else in the region. Most traditional

Karok twined basket, c. 1890; in the Denver Art Museum. Courtesy of the Denver Art Museum, Colorado

Chinook art is represented by just a few angular figures incised on mountain sheephorn bowls. In the southernmost part of the culture area, in northwestern California, art generally focused on geometric patterns incised on elkhorn objects and shells.

Weaving was also highly developed. The inner bark of red cedar was stripped, and the long ribbonlike strands were woven into mats and baskets, using a checkerwork technique. The same material could be shredded into finely divided flexible hanks, which were twined together to make a slip-on rain cape shaped like a truncated cone. The softer inner bark of yellow cedar was made into robes. Persons of high status wore robes made of or edged with strips of sea otter fur and yarn made of the wool of mountain goats. Salish groups near the Georgia Strait wove robes of mountain goat wool and also of wool from a special breed of shaggy dog. The Chilkat, a Tlingit group, wove robes and basketry, applying various twilling techniques to fabric and basketry alike. Their blankets bore representations of crests in blue, yellow, black, and white.

Twined basketry made from long flexible splints split from spruce roots illustrated great technical skill. Baskets so tightly woven as to be waterproof were made for cooking in northern and northwestern California. Their contents were boiled by placing hot stones into the soup or potage within the basket. Storage containers, receptacles for valuables large and small, and rain hats were also woven. The Coast Salish specialty was coiled baskets.

Dress patterns of the area were fairly simple, and, although ceremonial garments and some hats could be highly embellished, most clothing was worn for protection from the environment rather than for ostentatious display. Both women and men customarily wore some combination of necklaces, earrings, nose rings, bracelets, and anklets. These were made of various materials, mostly shells, copper, wood, and fur. Some individuals rubbed grease and ochre onto their skin to produce a red colour, often accented with black. Tattooing was also practiced. Throughout the region women wore skirts or gowns of buckskin, soft leather, or woven wool or plant fibres. Men's dress varied from tribe to tribe but was in general quite minimal—most men wore nothing but ornaments on warm days. Men of the northernmost Tlingit and the Kitksan of the upper Skeena wore tailored buckskin breechcloths, leggings, and shirts in cold weather. Elsewhere they wore robes of yellow cedar bark or pelts in cold weather and rain capes in downpours.

FAMILY MATTERS

Northern province peoples were matrilineal: they passed rank, land, and instruction through the mother. The other three provinces, however, tended to be patrilineal. Parents typically arranged most marriages, openly vying to ensure that their children rose in status (or maintained their current standing). As with up-marrying slaves, members of the middle classes of a group could marry up if they had distinguished themselves in some way. The children of these marriages would inherit the status of the higher-ranking spouse. If the spouse of lower rank was not distinguished in some way, the children would accrue the lower status. As this was generally seen as an undesirable outcome, such matches occurred relatively rarely.

An interesting aspect of Northwest Coast culture was the emphasis on teaching children etiquette, moral standards, and other traditions of social import. Every society has processes by which children are taught the behaviour proper to their future roles, but often such teaching is not an overt or deliberate process. On the Northwest Coast, however, particularly northward of the Columbia River, children

RAVEN CYCLE LEGENDS

Native Americans from the Northwest Coast between Alaska and British Columbia were the originators of a group of trickster-transformer legends known as the Raven cycle. These traditional tales feature Raven as a culture hero, who was sometimes ingenious and sometimes dull. This bird-human's voracious hunger, greed, and erotic appetite give rise to violent and amorous adventures that explain how the world of humans came to be.

As with the trickster-transformer tales of other cultures, stories about Raven often begin with him instigating a crisis that precipitates social or physical chaos. The tales then recount the ultimate resolution of these crises (often at Raven's expense) and the re-creation of order out of chaos. The Raven cycle begins with a boy's birth and relates early adventures that include his seduction of his aunt (sometimes replaced by the daughter of the Sky Chief) and subsequent flight to the sky to escape the flood that ensues from his transgression of incest (or status) rules. Raven, the result of this scandalous union, falls to earth during the flight. There Raven is adopted by a chief. As an adult, Raven transforms the earth from a dark and arid land inhabited by a variety of ferocious monsters into a land of rivers, lakes, and mountains inhabited by animals and human beings. He travels about changing aspects of the physical environment into their present forms, often through deception. The dozens of tales that recount his activities include Raven's impersonation of a woman to embarrass a man; his killing of a monster by putting hot stones down its throat; and his role as the "bungling host," a common motif of a guest who is fed by an animal wizard, then tries to imitate it in producing food but, lacking his host's magic, fails ignominiously. In other areas of North America, Mink, Blue Jay, Fox, or Coyote replace Raven as the hero of similar tales.

were instructed formally. This instruction began at an age when children were still in their cradles or toddling, and all elder relatives, particularly grandparents, participated in it. Lessons were often delivered gently and humorously through the telling and retelling of folktales. Trickster tales recounting Raven's exploits were especially entertaining, because his troubles were so obviously the result of his dissolute, lazy, gluttonous, and lecherous personality. Children born to high status were given formal instruction throughout childhood and adolescence. They had to learn not only routine etiquette but also the lengthy traditions by which the rank and privileges of their particular group were validated, including rituals, songs, and formulaic prayers.

Changes in status were generally marked by public ceremonies. Formal rituals were considered necessary at each of two or three critical stages in a person's lifetime—birth, a girl's attainment of puberty (there were no boys' puberty rites in the area), and death—because at those times the participants in these events might be especially vulnerable or so filled with power that they could inadvertently harm others. A newborn infant was believed to be in danger of harm by supernatural beings. The infant's parents were simultaneously in danger and potentially dangerous. Mystic forms of vulnerability and volatility also accrued to girls at puberty, to the close kin of a deceased person, and to those who prepared and disposed of the dead. Such perils were avoided by isolating the persons involved—either within a boarded-off cubicle in the house or in a simple structure out in the woods—and by limiting their diet to old dried fish and water. At the conclusion of the isolation period, a formal purification ritual was performed. The intensity of the restrictions varied considerably, not only in different parts of the coast but even within individual houses. Often the pubescent daughter of a chief, for example, was secluded for many months, whereas her low-ranking house sister might have to observe only a few days of confinement.

Over most of the coast there was an enormous fear of the dead. A body was usually removed from the house through some makeshift aperture other than the door and disposed of as rapidly as possible. An exception occurred in the northern province, where bodies of chiefs were placed in state for several days while clan dirges were sung. Disposal of the dead varied. In the northern province, cremation was practiced. In the Wakashan and part of the Coast Salish areas, large wooden coffins were suspended from the branches of tall trees or placed in rock shelters. Other Coast Salish deposited their dead in canoes set up on stakes. In southwestern Oregon and northwest California, interment in the ground was preferred.

RELIGIOUS BELIEFS AND PERFORMANCE

Numerous commonalities among religions of the Northwest Coast supply the broad foundation for a wide variety of religious ritual.

One concept was that salmon were supernatural beings who voluntarily assumed piscine form each year to sacrifice themselves for the benefit of humankind. On being caught, these spirit-beings returned to their home beneath the sea, where they were reincarnated if their bones or offal were returned to the water. If offended, however, they would refuse to return to the river. Hence, there were numerous specific prohibitions on acts believed to offend them and many observances designed to propitiate them, chief of which was the first-salmon ceremony. This rite varied in detail but invariably involved honouring the first salmon of the main fishing season by sprinkling them with eagle down, red ochre, or some other sacred substance, welcoming them in a formal speech, cooking them, and distributing their flesh, or morsels of it, communion-fashion, to all the members of the local group and any guests. The maximal elaboration of this rite occurred in northwestern California in what have been called world-renewal ceremonies. These combined first-salmon rituals, first-fruits observances, and dances in which lineage wealth was displayed. Elsewhere the first-salmon rituals were less elaborate but still important, except among the Tlingit, who did not perform them.

Another religious concept was the acquisition of personal power by seeking individual contact with a spirit-being, usually through prayer and a vision. Among Coast Salish all success in life—whether in hunting, woodworking, accumulating wealth, military ventures, or magic—was bestowed by spirit-beings encountered in the vision quest. From these entities each person acquired songs, special regalia, and dances. Collectively, the dances constituted the major ceremonials of the Northwest Coast peoples. Known as the spirit dances, they were performed during the winter months.

In the Wakashan and northern provinces, it was believed that remote ancestors who had undertaken vision quests had been rewarded with totemic symbols or crests. Displaying these hereditary crests and recounting the traditions of their acquisition formed an important part of potlatches. In the Wakashan area certain ceremonial cycles called for the dramatization of the whole tale of the supernatural encounter, which in some cases included the spirit-being's possession of and its eventual exorcism from the seeker. Such dramas were performed by dancing societies.

Shamanism differed from other acquisitions of supernatural power only in the nature of the power obtained—that is, power to heal the sick through extraction of disease objects or recovery of a strayed soul. It was commonly believed that some shamans, or medicine men and women, had the power to cause infirmities as well as to cure them. Witchcraft was used to kill others or make them ill and was believed to be carried out by malicious persons who knew secret rituals for that purpose.

CULTURAL COHESION AND ADJUSTMENT

European and Euro-American colonialism affected the Northwest Coast peoples differently depending on the period and the region. The Tlingit were the first group to encounter such outsiders, when Russian traders made landfall in Tlingit territory in 1741. These colonizers did not establish a garrison in the region until 1799 and then only after heated resistance. Spain sent parties to the Haida in 1774, Britain to the Nuu-chah-nulth in 1778, and the United States to various groups about 1800.

EARLY TRADE

The colonial expeditions sought sea otter pelts, which were particularly dense and highly prized in the lucrative Chinese market. Although the Russians pressed Aleut men into corvée labour as sea otter hunters, they traded with Northwest Coast peoples for furs and food. In exchange they brought foreign manufactured goods to the tribes. These materials affected indigenous cultures only slightly, as the tribes selected the articles that complemented existing culture patterns. They acquired steel blades, for example, that could be fitted to traditional adzes to cut more efficiently than stone or shell blades, yet initially spurned axe and hatchet blades because these required a drastic change in motor habits and coordination patterns.

By the middle of the 19th century, a number of trading posts had been established in the region. The peoples of the region recognized that fur traders were more interested in commerce than in self-sufficiency. Having long been involved in commerce among themselves, indigenous groups found novel ways to profit from this. Tlingit house groups provisioned the trading posts with fish, game, and potatoes. The latter were a South American crop that had by this time circled the globe, having arrived in the Northwest Coast via Russian trade. They sold literally tons of food. Records indicate that in 1847, for instance, the Russians purchased more than 83,000 pounds (37,650 kg) of game and fish plus more than 35,000 pounds (nearly 16,000 kg) of potatoes from the Tlingit. Other avenues of entrepreneurship were open as well. The Tsimshian and others gained control of major portage routes and shipping lanes, demanding fees for passage and vessel rental. Some of their monopolies were in place for decades. Still other groups hired out their slaves as prostitutes or labourers.

THE SETTLEMENT MOVEMENT

Although the Northwest Coast tribes had quickly found ways to benefit from maritime trade, they found it more difficult to cope with the flood of settlers from the eastern United States and Canada that began in the 1840s. These emigrant farmers were encouraged by their governments to move to what are now western Washington, Oregon, Vancouver Island, and the lower Fraser River valley. In the United States this occupation was accompanied by the removal of the tribes to small reservations in present-day Washington and Oregon, under the provisions of formal treaties. In the area that is now British Columbia, there were no treaties extinguishing native title to the land. Undeveloped land was presumed to belong to the crown, and transfers of developed land were private affairs.

Effective missionary activity began in various parts of the coast in conjunction with the settlement movement. Missionaries on the Northwest Coast were quite successful at directing culture change, teaching not only Christian precepts but also the precepts of etiquette, sobriety, household hygiene, and punctuality and a host

The Fraser River valley, British Columbia, Canada. Shutterstock.com

of other requirements for competency in the dominant culture. In addition, the formal schooling of indigenous children was in the hands of missionaries on much of the coast for several decades.

Effects of Settlement: Disease and Misunderstanding

From the late 18th through the entire 19th century, the most disruptive events for Northwest Coast peoples were epidemics of contagious diseases such as smallpox, venereal infections, and measles. These had a profound effect on native society because—never having been exposed to these illnesses before—the people suffered extremely high death rates. It is estimated that between 1780 and 1900 the indigenous population in the region declined by as much as 80 percent. Depopulation forced societies into

unusual distributions of roles and status positions. These
frequently involved adoptions, the allocation of multiple
titles to a single individual, and other compromises that
helped to maintain the social system despite rapid population decline. A great deal of ritual and practical knowledge
was lost when those who would have passed the information on grew ill and died.

By the second half of the 19th century, trading profits
had combined with high mortality and social uncertainty
to create increasingly extravagant potlatches. As houses
consolidated in response to losses from epidemics, some
used this traditional means of display to climb the status
hierarchy, while other houses engaged in lavish potlatches
to reaffirm or defend their high status. In addition, spirit
dancing seems to have become more extravagant and evoc-
ative. Unfortunately, both activities were misunderstood
by missionaries and government officials—potlatches
were seen as foolish "giveaways" that impoverished their
host families, while the reenactment of a legend of can-
nibalism within the spirit dance was misunderstood as the
actual consumption of human flesh. As a result, both practices were outlawed in Canada from 1884 to 1951, though
they persisted in discreet settings.

THE COLLAPSE OF THE FUR TRADE AND RISE OF THE SALMON INDUSTRY

In the closing decades of the 19th century, the fur trade
collapsed, and the peoples of the Northwest Coast found
themselves in dire economic straits. Divested of most of
their lands and increasingly dependent upon manufactured
goods, they needed to develop new economic resources.
Indigenous reasons for the accumulation of wealth differed from those of Euro-Americans, but, as before,
the tribes found ways to enter the dominant economic

system. Some individuals began by working for wages in a dull day-after-day routine, something that most other Native American peoples refused to do. At first there was less hired work available than potential employees. Jobs were mostly limited to guiding prospectors, backpacking cargo over mountain passes, cutting cordwood for coastal steamers, and working as farm and domestic labour. Yet when the canned salmon industry developed, principally from the Fraser River northward, wage labour boomed.

Native peoples knew more about the habits of the region's salmon population than anyone else. This presented them with a clear advantage, especially given that the commercial salmon fishery began with a simple technology. The Northwest Coast Indians had long used canoes, spears, nets, and weirs, and over the decades most changes in the fishing industry involved increased mechanization rather than changes in its fundamental premises: motive power changed from paddles and oars to two-cycle gasoline engines, high-speed gasoline engines, and eventually diesel engines. Harvesting tools changed from gill nets and crude beach seines to huge purse seines handled with power gear. And navigation changed from dead reckoning to a reliance on tide tables, compasses, and charts. Native American fishers (both men and women) learned the new skills alongside their coworkers, and a number eventually became independent operators. Often these individuals were of hereditary high status and fulfilled traditional expectations for behaviour by employing, feeding, or otherwise aiding the lower status members of their house group. At the same time, native people, especially women, were employed in processing the catch—again activities to which they had long been accustomed. Fishing continues to be a mainstay of the economy in this region, and in the long run the indigenous peoples who depend on the industry face problems common to all commercial fishers:

commitment to a short-season industry that ties up capital in expensive boats and nets, seasonal income fluctuation, the potential for accidents, the prospect of overfishing, and the fickle nature of the market.

ORGANIZING AND LAND CLAIMS

Having retained a high level of economic independence relative to other North American groups, the peoples of this region were able to organize relatively effectively against government interference. Beginning in 1912, the Tlingit, Haida, and other tribes in southeastern Alaska created political groups called Native Brotherhoods, and in 1923 Native Sisterhoods, to act on behalf of the people in legal and other proceedings. Similar groups were subsequently formed in coastal British Columbia. These organizations provided valuable training in modern political processes and negotiations. Their successes are remarkable, given the rampant discrimination faced by indigenous peoples of the region, where some businesses posted signs with statements such as "No natives or dogs allowed" as recently as the 1940s.

The Native Brotherhoods (and the nascent, but not yet chartered, Sisterhoods) pursued a variety of legal strategies to ensure equal treatment under the law, beginning with the 1915 passage of an act granting territorial citizenship to Native Alaskans who met certain criteria. In 1922 they won the acquittal of a traditional leader who had been arrested for voting in the Alaska primary elections, an important precursor to legislation granting U.S. citizenship to all native peoples in 1924 (Canadian federal elections were opened to native peoples in 1960). Also in 1924 a prominent Native Brotherhood leader and lawyer, William L. Paul, Sr. (Tlingit), became the first indigenous person elected to Alaska's territorial legislature.

These victories were followed by a variety of successful antidiscrimination suits and land claims. In the United States the latter were ultimately resolved through the Alaska Native Claims Settlement Act of 1971. This act resolved indigenous claims of illegal takings in Alaska and created a series of for-profit corporations charged with managing a final settlement of some 44 million acres (17.8 million hectares) of land and $962 million. Native peoples participate in these corporations as shareholders, directors, and employees. The Canadian organizations effected the repeal, in 1951, of laws prohibiting potlatches and the filing of land claims. After many years of discussion, the provincial government of British Columbia agreed in 1990 to negotiate tribal land claims through a body known as the British Columbia Treaty Commission. The prescribed negotiation process was necessarily painstaking, and the first Agreement-in-Principal between a tribe and the government was signed in 1999. At the turn of the 21st century, progress remained slow and a number of tribal claims remained in negotiation with the Treaty Commission.

The peoples of the Northwest Coast had rich and reliable supplies of salmon and other fish, as well as a variety of sea mammals, shellfish, birds, and wild food plants. The resource base was so abundant that they alone among nonagricultural peoples created highly stratified societies of hereditary elites, commoners, and slaves. Most groups constructed villages near waterways or the coast. Each village also had land rights to an upland territory. Dwellings were rectilinear structures built of timbers or planks and were usually quite large because the members of a corporate "house" typically lived together in one building. Northwest Coast cultures are known for their fine wood and stone carvings, large and seaworthy watercraft, memorial or totem poles, and basketry.

BELLA COOLA

The Bella Coola, who call themselves Nuxalk, traditionally inhabited the area that includes the present-day central British Columbia coast, the length of the upper channels of Dean and Burke and the lower Bella Coola River valley areas. The language they used was Salishan, which was related to the southern Coast Salish. Their ancestors almost certainly split from the main body of Salish and migrated northward. Although their material culture, ceremonials, and mythology resembled those of their Heiltsuq (Kwakiutl) neighbours, their social organization was similar to that of the more distant Salish.

Traditionally, the Bella Coola inhabited permanent villages of large plank-built houses occupied by a number of families. They used wood for houses, canoes, and watertight boxes that served a variety of domestic purposes. Cedar bark provided fibres for clothing, baskets were made of cedar and spruce, and alder and cedar were carved into masks and other ceremonial objects, including spectacular totem poles. Fish was their basic food source, supplemented by hunting and by collecting wild plant foods. Salmon, taken in the summer, were eaten fresh or smoked. Oil extracted from eulachon (candlefish) was used as a condiment. Life was organized on a village basis, with status dependent on both hereditary rank and wealth, measured by ostentatious giving at potlatches. No formal political structure connected Bella Coola communities to one another, but they had a strong feeling of shared identity based on common language, common origin, and cultural pride. Secret societies were important, with an unusually well-developed pantheon of deities and great emphasis on numerous oral traditions.

The Bella Coola probably numbered about 5,000 at the time of their first contacts with Europeans. Disease in the 19th century reduced their numbers to fewer than 1,000 people, most living in a single village. Bella Coola descendants numbered some 3,000 in the early 21st century.

CHINOOK

The Chinook spoke Chinookan languages and traditionally inhabited the areas presently known as Washington and Oregon, between the Columbia River's mouth and The Dalles. Renowned for their trading, they had associations with people as far away as the Great Plains. The Columbia was a main indigenous thoroughfare, and the Chinooks' position facilitated contact with northern and southern coastal peoples as well as with interior groups. The river was a rich source of salmon, the basis of the regional economy, and many groups traded with the Chinook for dried fish. Other important trade items were slaves from California, Nuu-chah-nulth (Nootka) canoes, and dentalium shells, which were highly valued as hair and clothing ornaments. Chinook Jargon, the trade language of the Northwest Coast, was a combination of Chinook with Nuu-chah-nulth and other Native American, English, and French terms. Chinook Jargon may have originated before European contact. It was used across a broad territory reaching from California to Alaska.

The Chinook were first described ethnographically by the American explorers Lewis and Clark in 1805. Because American colonialism severely disrupted Chinook culture, ultimately removing the people to reservations, most information about traditional Chinook life is based on the records of these and other traders and explorers, together with what is known of neighbouring groups.

The tribe's basic social unit was probably a local group consisting of close relatives and headed by a senior member. Traditional Chinook religion focused on the first-salmon rite, a ritual in which each group welcomed the annual salmon run. Another important ritual was the individual vision quest, an ordeal undertaken by all male and some female adolescents to acquire a guardian spirit that would give them hunting, curing, or other powers, bring them good luck, or teach them songs and dances. Singing ceremonies were public demonstrations of these gifts. The Chinook also had potlatches, which were ceremonial distributions of property.

Early 21st-century population estimates indicated more than 1,500 Chinook descendants.

COAST SALISH

Salish speakers who reside throughout what are currently the Strait of Georgia, Puget Sound, southern Vancouver Island, a great deal of the Olympic Peninsula, and nearly all of western Washington state are commonly known as the Coast Salish. The Tillamook were a Salish group who lived south of Oregon's Columbia River. The Bella Coola, a group dwelling more to the north in British Columbia, likely migrated from the main body of Coast Salish. The Coast Salish probably migrated to the coast from the interior, where other Salish-speakers lived. They were culturally similar to the Chinook.

Like other Northwest Coast Indians before colonial contact, the Coast Salish lived principally on fish, although some groups living along the upper rivers relied more heavily on hunting. They built permanent winter houses of wood and used mat lodges for temporary camps.

Traditionally, the tribe's basic social unit was the local group consisting of close relatives. Each extended family usually lived in one large house, and groups of houses formed a winter village. People dispersed during the summer for fishing, hunting, and berrying.

One of the most important Coast Salish events was the potlatch. Potlatches enabled the host or sponsor to acquire or maintain prestige. Elaborate ceremonies held during the winter included dances inspired by spirits in dreams or trances. Many other forms of performance art were treated as property to which individuals or groups acquired exclusive rights by inheritance, marriage, or purchase.

Early 21st-century population estimates indicated more than 25,000 Coast Salish descendants in Canada and the United States.

HAIDA

The Haida-speaking peoples called the Haida settled in what are now known as the Queen Charlotte Islands, British Columbia, Can. The Alaskan Haida—who inhabit the southern part of Prince of Wales Island, Alaska, U.S.— are called Kaigani. Haida culture is related to the cultures of the neighbouring Tlingit and Tsimshian.

Traditional Haida social organization was built around two major subdivisions, or moieties. Moiety membership was assigned at birth and based on maternal affiliation. Each moiety consisted of many local segments or lineages, which owned rights to economically important lands, occupied separate villages, and had their own primary chiefs (a village's highest ranking member) and lesser house chiefs. Each lineage functioned independently of the others in matters of war, peace, religion, and economics.

Traditional Haida economics were based on fishing (especially of salmon, halibut, and cod) and hunting. The annual salmon run offered the Haida and other Northwest Coast Indians a productive and reliable resource that required relatively little investment on their part, thus supporting the tribe's artistic and ceremonial pursuits. The Haida were widely known for their art and architecture, both of which focused on the creative embellishment of

Wooden thunderbird of the Haida people; Northwest Coast of North America, 19th century; in the British Museum, London. Courtesy of the trustees of the British Museum

wood. They decorated utilitarian objects with depictions of supernatural and other beings in a highly conventionalized style. They also produced elaborate totem poles with carved and painted crests. Fine examples of traditional Haida arts and architecture may be seen at the Haida Heritage Centre at Kaay Llnagaay, near the town of Skidegate in the Queen Charlotte Islands.

Haida ceremonial culture was most fully expressed in potlatches, which were held to confer, validate, or uphold political rank, such as chieftainship, or social status. Potlatches were also given to mark events such as house building, totem-pole raising, and funerals and for purposes such as saving face.

Early 21st-century population estimates indicated more than 20,000 Haida descendants.

NUANCES OF THE TOTEM POLE

The vertically mounted, carved, and painted logs called totem poles are constructed by the aboriginal peoples of the Northwest Coast of North America. Totem poles fall into seven main categoies: memorial, or heraldic, poles, erected when a house changes hands to commemorate the past owner and to identify the present one; grave markers (tombstones); house posts, which support the roof; portal poles, which have a hole through which a person enters the house; welcoming poles, placed at the edge of a body of water to identify the owner of the waterfront; mortuary poles, in which the remains of the deceased are placed; and ridicule poles, on which an important individual who had failed in some way had his likeness carved upside down.

The carving on totem poles separates and emphasizes the flat, painted surfaces of the symbolic animals and spirits depicted on them. Each pole generally has from one (as with a grave marker) to many (as with a family legend) animal images on it, all following standardized forms that are familiar to all Indians of

Totem pole from Kitwancool Creek, B.C., Can. W.E. Ferguson/
Shostal Associates

the Northwest Coast. Beavers, for example, always include cross-
hatched tails, and eagles show downward curved beaks.

The word *totem* refers to a guardian or ancestral being, usually supernatural, that is revered and respected, but not always
worshipped. The significance of the real or mythological animal
carved on a totem pole is its identification with the lineage of
the head of the household. The animal is displayed as a type of
family crest, much as an Englishman might have a lion on his
crest, or a rancher a bull on his brand. More widely known, but in
fact far less common, are the elaborately carved tall totem poles
that relate an entire family legend in the form of a pictograph.
This legend is not something that can be read in the usual sense

of the word. Only with an understanding of what the symbols mean to the Indians and a knowledge of the history and customs of the clan involved can the pole be interpreted. Each animal or spirit carved on the pole has meaning, and when combined on the pole in sequence, each figure is an important symbol constituent of a story or myth. An exact interpretation of any set of symbols, however, would be almost impossible without the help of a knowledgeable narrator from the family.

The totem pole was also a sign of the owner's affluence because hiring an artist to make a pole was expensive. Totem pole carving reached its peak in the early and middle 19th century, when the introduction of good metal tools and the wealth gained from the fur trade made it possible for many chiefs to afford these displays. Few examples of this period remain, however, as the moist coastal atmosphere causes the cedar poles to rot and fall in about 60 to 70 years.

HUPA

The Hupa resided by the side of the lower Trinity River in what is now the state of California. They spoke an Athabaskan language also called Hupa. The Hupa merged facets of the Northwest Coast Indian and California Indian traditions.

Hupa villages tended to be located on the riverbank and included dwellings for women and children, separate semisubterranean buildings where men slept and took sweat baths, and small menstrual lodges for women. The Hupa economy was based on elk, deer, salmon, and acorns, all of which were readily available in the region. Fine basketry was made by twining segments of certain roots, leaves, and stems around prepared shoots. As an inland group, the Hupa often exchanged acorns and other local foods with the coast-dwelling Yurok, who reciprocated with redwood canoes, saltwater fish, mussels, and

Hupa female shaman, photograph by Edward S. Curtis, c. *1923.* Edward S. Curtis Collection/Library of Congress, Washington, D.C. (neg. no. LC-USZ62-101261)

seaweed. Members of the two tribes attended each other's ceremonies and sometimes intermarried.

Hupa people traditionally measured wealth in terms of the ownership of woodpecker scalps and dentalium shells, the latter of which were probably received in trade from the Yurok. The village's richest man was its headman. His power and his property passed to his son, but anyone who acquired more property might obtain the dignity and power of that office. Personal insult, injury, or homicide were usually settled through the payment of blood money.

The recitation of magical formulas was an important part of traditional Hupa religion. Shamanism was also common. Shamans' fees were paid in dentalium shells or deerskin blankets. Three major dances were held annually for the benefit of the community, as were spring and fall ceremonial feasts.

Early 21st-century population estimates indicated more than 3,000 Hupa descendants.

KWAKIUTL

The Kwakiutl people call themselves Kwakwaka'wakw, which is translated "those who speak Kwakwala." Traditionally, they inhabited the shorelines between what is now Vancouver Island and the mainland in British Columbia. The Wakashan language they speak consists of three major dialects: Haisla, spoken on the Gardner Canal and Douglas Channel; Heiltsuq, spoken from Gardner Canal to Rivers Inlet; and southern Kwakiutl, spoken from Rivers Inlet to Cape Mudge on the mainland and the northern end of Vancouver Island. The Kwakiutl are culturally and linguistically related to the Nuu-chah-nulth (or Nootka).

The Kwakiutl contributed extensively to the early development of anthropology as the subjects of ethnographic studies by pioneering scholar Franz Boas. In more than 5,000 pages written over almost half a century, Boas described and analyzed nearly every aspect of Kwakiutl culture and its relationships to other Northwest Coast

Indians with whom the tribe shared general features of technology, economy, art, myths, and religion.

Traditionally, the Kwakiutl subsisted mainly by fishing and had a technology based on woodworking. Their society was stratified by rank, which was determined primarily by the inheritance of names and privileges. The latter could include the right to sing certain songs, use certain crests, and wear particular ceremonial masks.

The potlatch was elaborately developed by the southern Kwakiutl. Their potlatches were often combined with performances by dancing societies, each society having a series of dances that dramatized ancestral interactions with supernatural beings. These beings were portrayed as giving gifts of ceremonial prerogatives such as songs, dances, and names, which became hereditary property.

Early 21st-century population estimates indicated approximately 700 individuals of Kwakiutl descent.

Kwakiutl performers in ceremonial dance attire, c. *1914.* Edward S. Curtis—Edward S. Curtis Collection/Library of Congress, Washington, D.C. (digital. id. cph 3c08464)

NUU-CHAH-NULTH

Perhaps better known as Nootka, the Nuu-chah-nulth (which means "along the mountains") speak a language called Wakashan. Culturally speaking, the Nuu-chah-nulth are related to the Kwakiutl. The Nitinat groups inhabit the southwest coast of Vancouver Island. Bands of the Makah reside on Cape Flattery, the northwest tip of the state of Washington

Traditionally, local groups in the central and southern Nuu-chah-nulth regions were socially and politically independent. In northern areas they usually formed larger tribes with large winter villages. There were also several confederacies of tribes, dating to prehistoric times, that shared summer villages and fishing and hunting grounds near the coast. The Nuu-chah-nulth moved seasonally to areas of economic importance, returning to their principal villages during the winter when subsistence activity slowed.

Like several other Northwest Coast Indians, the Nuu-chah-nulth were whale hunters, employing special equipment such as large dugout canoes and harpoons with long lines and sealskin floats. The whale harpooner was a person of high rank, and families passed down the magical and practical secrets that made for successful hunting. There was also a whale ritualist who, by appropriate ceremonial procedures, caused whales that had died of natural causes to drift ashore. Many features of this whaling complex suggest ancient ties with Eskimo and Aleut cultures.

Before the Nuu-chah-nulth were colonized by Russia, England, Canada, and the United States, their religion centred on shamanism and animism. The most important Nuu-chah-nulth ceremony was the shamans' dance, a reenactment of the kidnapping of an ancestor by supernatural beings who later gave him supernatural gifts and released him. The ceremony served to define each individual's place in the social order. The public performance ended with a potlatch.

Early 21st-century population estimates indicated some 8,500 individuals of Nuu-chah-nulth descent.

TLINGIT

Of all the Northwest Coast Indians, the Tlingit reside the furthest to the north. They inhabit southern Alaska's coasts and islands between Yakutat Bay and Cape Fox. According to their traditions, some of their ancestors came from the south and others migrated to the coast from the Canadian interior. Their language is also called Tlingit.

Traditional Tlingit society included three levels of kinship organization. Every individual belonged to one of two moieties, the largest kin group. Each moiety comprised several clans, and the members of a given clan attributed their origin to a common legendary ancestor. The most basic and important organizational level was the lineage, an extended family group related through maternal descent. Each lineage was essentially self-sufficient: it owned a specific territory, could conduct ceremonies, was politically independent, and had its own leaders. There was rarely a leader or authority over the entire tribe. Lineages might cooperate during periods of war and choose a temporary leader for that purpose, but there was no compulsion to join such alliances. During the historic period there was a tendency for two or more lineages to consolidate into unified villages, but before contact with Europeans each lineage probably had its own village.

The traditional Tlingit economy was based on fishing, and salmon was the main source of food. The Tlingit also hunted sea, and sometimes land, mammals. Wood was

Tlingit totem pole and community house in Totem Bight State Park, Ketchikan, Alaska. Bob and Ira Spring

the primary material for manufacture and was used for houses, memorial (totem) poles, canoes, dishes, utensils, and other objects. Large permanent houses were built near good fishing grounds and safe landing places for canoes, often along the beaches of a bay sheltered from the tides. These houses were winter residences. During the summer, inhabitants dispersed to take advantage of more distant fishing and hunting grounds. Potlatches marked a cycle of rituals mourning the death of a lineage chief.

Early 21st-century population estimates indicated some 22,000 individuals of Tlingit descent.

TSIMSHIAN

By tradition, the Tsimshian (also spelled Chimmesyan) peoples speak a Penutian language called Tsimshian, which includes three dialects. Niska is spoken along the Nass River. All along the lower Skeena and the coast, the people speak coastal Tsimshian. Finally, Kitksan (or Gitksan) is the language spoken along the upper Skeena. The Tsimshian settled on the mainland and islands around the Skeena and Nass rivers and Milbanke Sound in what is now British Columbia and Alaska.

The traditional economy of the Tsimshian was based on fishing. They passed the summer months trapping migrating salmon and eulachon (candlefish), a species of smelt. Eulachon were particularly valuable for their oil, which was made into a food highly regarded by many peoples of the area. Large permanent winter houses, made of wood and often carved and painted, symbolized the wealth of Tsimshian families. During the winter months, some land animals were also hunted.

The coastal Tsimshian and the Niska were divided into four major clans, or kin groups, the Kitksan into three. These were further divided into local segments or lineages, descent being traced through the maternal line. Each lineage was generally an independent social and ceremonial unit with its own fishing and hunting areas, berry grounds, house or houses, and heraldic crests representing events in the family history, as well as its own chiefs. Local groupings, or tribes, were composed of several lineages. Each lineage was ranked relative to the others, and the chief of the highest-ranked lineage was recognized as chief of the tribe. The tribe as a whole held properties such as the winter village site and participated in ceremonies and warfare.

The Tsimshian were known for their highly conventionalized applied art. Carved and painted totem poles were erected, primarily as memorials to deceased chiefs. The major Tsimshian potlatches had as their purpose the announcement and validation of the position of the new chief. Potlatches could also mark a series of events several years apart, such as house building, totem-pole raising, and dramatizations of privileges and crests.

Early 21st-century population estimates indicated some 5,000 Tsimshian descendants.

WIYOT

The Wiyot, the southernmost of the Northwest Coast Indians, lived along the lower Mad River, Humboldt Bay, and lower Eel River of what is now California and spoke Wiyot, an Algic (Algonquian-Ritwan) language. They were culturally and linguistically related to the Yurok and had some cultural elements typical of the California Indians to their immediate south.

Traditional Wiyot settlements were located on streams or bays, fairly close to the ocean. The Wiyot rarely ventured onto the ocean for subsistence or for travel, preferring still water. Villages consisted of 4 to 12 plank houses. There were also scattered hamlets of one or two houses. In addition, there were men's sweathouses, used for sleeping, working, and leisure as well as for regular sweat baths and purification.

Before colonization the Wiyot were mainly fishers, catching salmon and other fish. They also collected mollusks, especially clams, and trapped land mammals. Houses and canoes were made of coast redwood. The Wiyot economy used dentalium shells, long obsidian knives, woodpecker scalps, and white deerskins as symbols of wealth. There were no formal chiefs or individuals vested with significant political authority, but wealthy men were influential as advisers. Disputes, and even murder, were settled by the payment of dentalium shells as blood money.

Shamanism was important in Wiyot culture, and most Wiyot shamans were women. They were thought to acquire their powers on mountaintops at night. Some shamans only diagnosed disease. Others cured by sucking out disease objects and blood. Traditional religious beliefs included a creator-god and many animal characters.

Early 21st-century population estimates indicated some 700 individuals of Wiyot descent.

YUROK

The Yurok traditionally inhabited the areas presently known as California along the lower Klamath River and the coast of the Pacific Ocean. Because their territory lay on the boundary flanked by differing cultural and ecological areas, the Yurok combined the typical subsistence practices of Northwest Coast Indians with many religious and organizational features common to California Indians. The Yurok used an Algic (Algonquian-Ritwan) language and were culturally and linguistically related to the Wiyot.

Traditional Yurok villages were small collections of independent houses owned by individual families. Avoiding unified communities and an overall political authority, village residents sometimes shared rights to general subsistence areas and to the performance of certain rituals. Other rights, such as the right to use specific areas for fishing, hunting, and gathering, generally belonged to particular houses. These rights were acquired by inheritance or dowry, as part of blood money settlements, or by sale. In addition to dwellings, villages had sweat houses, each of which served as a gathering places for the men of an extended patrilineal family. There were also separate shelters where women withdrew during menstruation.

The traditional Yurok economy focused on salmon and acorns. The people also produced excellent basketry and made canoes from redwood trees, selling them to inland tribes. Wealth was counted in strings of dentalium shells, obsidian blades, woodpecker scalps, and albino deerskins. Acquiring wealth was an important goal in Yurok culture. Feuds were common, and payments of blood money were precisely defined according to the seriousness of the offense. The value of a human life depended on social status.

Traditional Yurok religion was concerned with an individual's effort to elicit supernatural aid, especially through ritual cleanliness, and with rituals for the public welfare. The tribe did not practice the potlatch, masked dances, representative carving, and other features typical of their Northwest Coast neighbours. The major ceremonies were those of the World Renewal cycle, which ensured an abundance of food, riches, and general well-being. This cycle included the recitation of magical formulas, repeating the words of an ancient spirit race, and other acts. The spiritual power to cure disease was granted only to women, giving these shamans prestige and a source of wealth.

Early 21st-century population estimates indicated some 6,000 individuals of Yurok descent.

CONCLUSION

This book has considered the location, climate, environment, languages, tribes, and common cultural characteristics of the three northernmost of the 10 culture areas of aboriginal North America: the Arctic region, which is near and above the Arctic Circle and includes the northernmost parts of present-day Alaska and Canada, as well as Greenland; the Subarctic region, which lies south of the Arctic and encompasses most of present-day Alaska and most of Canada, excluding the Maritime Provinces (New Brunswick, Nova Scotia, and Prince Edward Island; these are part of the Northeast culture area); and the Northwest Coast, which is bounded on the west by the Pacific Ocean and on the east by the Coast Range, the Sierra Nevada, and the Rocky Mountains. Among the peoples of these culture areas are many commonalities but also many differences that date from their earliest history. This book has also sought to give some notion of what life was like before and after the incursion of European settlers, with what scientist and writer Jared Diamond has called "guns, germs, and steel." The questions raised by the initial contact between native peoples and these settlers, as well as by the ongoing relationship between these two groups, are both simple and profound.

GLOSSARY

aegis Controlling or conditioning influence.

ameliorate To make better or more tolerable.

animism Belief in innumerable spiritual beings concerned with human affairs and capable of helping or harming human interests.

anorak A usually pullover hooded jacket long enough to cover the hips.

assimilation The process whereby individuals or groups of differing ethnic heritage are absorbed into the dominant culture of a society.

atlatl A device for throwing a spear or dart that consists of a rod or board with a projection (as a hook) at the rear end to hold the weapon in place until released.

band A small, egalitarian, group of people, a subsidiary unit of a tribe.

corvée Type of labour exacted by public authorities in place of taxation.

dirge A song or hymn of grief or lamentation.

docility The quality or state of being easily led or managed.

endogamy Marriage within a specific group as required by custom or law.

ethnography The study and systematic recording of human cultures.

ethnonym The name that an ethnic group ascribes to themselves.

exogamy Marriage outside of a specific group as required by custom or law.

hinterland A region lying inland from a coast or remote from urban areas.

igloo A form of shelter used in Arctic regions usually made of wood, sod, or stone when permanent or of blocks of snow or ice in the form of a dome when built for temporary use.

kashim A large subterranean house inhabited by Yupik men; also used for ceremonies.

kayak An Eskimo (Inuit) canoe originally made of a frame covered with skins except for a small opening in the centre and propelled by a double-bladed paddle.

levirate The sometimes compulsory marriage of a man to his brother's widow wherein he became responsible for providing for her and her children.

manitou A supernatural force that according to an Algonquian conception pervades the natural world.

menarche The beginning of menstruation; a girl's first menstrual period.

moiety A tribal subdivision that has a complementary counterpart.

nomenclature Name or designation.

parka A hooded fur pullover garment for Arctic wear.

patrilineal Relating to, based on, or tracing descent through the father's line.

phratry A tribal subdivision; specifically, an exogamous group typically comprising several totemic clans.

plebiscite A vote by which the people of an entire tribe, region, or country vote for or against a proposal, especially when choosing a government or ruler.

potlatch A ceremonial feast of the American Indians of the Northwest Coast marked by the host's lavish distribution of gifts or sometimes destruction of property to demonstrate wealth and generosity with the expectation of eventual reciprocation.

referendum The principle or practice of submitting to popular vote a measure passed on or proposed by a legislative body or by popular initiative.

ribaldry Language that is characterized by or makes use of coarse, indecent humour.

séance A spiritualist meeting to receive spirit communications.

shaman A priest or priestess who has shown an exceptionally strong affinity with the spirit world. Shamans are also considered healers and are thought to be adept at divination.

taiga A biome where the land is covered by conifers and lichen, and the climate is harsh and cold.

umiak An open Eskimo (Inuit) boat originally made of a wooden frame covered with hide.

unglaciated Not frozen.

vernacular Using a language or dialect native to a region or country rather than a literary, cultured, or foreign language.

vicissitude A favourable or unfavourable event or situation that occurs by chance.

wickiup A dome-shaped form of lodging favoured by Northeast Native American peoples, constructed by draping bent saplings with rushes or bark.

yurt A circular domed tent of skins or felt stretched over a collapsible lattice framework and used by pastoral peoples of inner Asia.

BIBLIOGRAPHY

An excellent collection of photos and essays was commissioned to celebrate the opening of the Smithsonian Institution's National Museum of the American Indian, Gerald McMaster and Clifford E. Trafzer (eds.), *Native Universe: Voices of Indian America* (2004). An encyclopaedic summary of knowledge, literature, and research on the principal cultural regions north of Mexico is provided by the multivolume William C. Sturtevant (ed.), *Handbook of North American Indians*, notably volumes 5, on the Arctic (1984), 6, on the Subarctic (1981), and 7, on the Northwest Coast (1990). Other, special topical volumes in the series—such as volume 4, which treats the overall history of Indian-white relations—are also useful.

Regarding the peoples of the Arctic, Nelson H.H. Graburn and B. Stephen Strong, *Circumpolar Peoples: An Anthropological Perspective* (1973), provides a good general introduction. More recent works include Yuri Slezkine, *Arctic Mirrors: Russia and the Small Peoples of the North* (1994); Gretel Ehrlich, *In the Empire of Ice: Encounters in a Changing Landscape* (2010); Seth Kantner, *Shopping for Porcupine: A Life in Arctic Alaska* (2008); and John F. Hoffecker, *A Prehistory of the North: Human Settlement of the Higher Latitudes* (2005). Books discussing the special concerns of Arctic peoples include Mark Nuttall, *Protecting the Arctic: Indigenous Peoples and Cultural Survival* (1998); and Eric Alden Smith and Joan McCarter, *Contested Arctic: Indigenous Peoples, Industrial States, and the Circumpolar Environment* (1997). A fascinating book with pictures and essays about photography and photographers in the Arctic is J.C.H. King and Henrietta Lidchi (eds.), *Imaging the Arctic* (1998).

Keith J. Crowe, *A History of the Original Peoples of Northern Canada*, rev. ed. (1991), is a useful textbook on Subarctic peoples. Discussions of history include Shepard Krech III (ed.), *The Subarctic Fur Trade: Native Social and Economic Adaptations* (1984); Kerry Abel, *Drum Songs: Glimpses of Dene History* (1993), on the indigenous people of the McKenzie River drainage area; William E. Simeone, *Rifles, Blankets, and Beads: Identity, History, and the Northern Athapaskan Potlatch* (1995, reissued 2002); and Lucy Eldersveld Murphy, *A Gathering of Rivers: Indians, Métis, and Mining in the Western Great Lakes, 1737–1832* (2000). The real and potential impacts of change on 20th- and 21st-century Subarctic communities are the focus of a number of volumes. Two of these concern indigenous resistance to a major Canadian hydroelectric project: Ronald Niezen, *Defending the Land: Sovereignty and Forest Life in James Bay Cree Society* (1998); and Toby Morantz, *The White Man's Gonna Getcha: The Colonial Challenge to the Crees in Quebec* (2002). The sources of conflict within tribal communities in the Western Subarctic are examined in Kirk Dombrowski, *Against Culture: Development, Politics, and Religion in Indian Alaska* (2001). Also of interest are Colin Samson, *A Way of Life That Does Not Exist: Canada and the Extinguishment of the Innu* (2003); Kaneuketat and Georg Henriksen, *I Dreamed the Animals: Kaniuekutat: The Life of an Innu Hunter* (2009); Dennis Banks and Richard Erdoes, *Ojibwa Warrior: Dennis Banks and the Rise of the American Indian Movement* (2004); and Brenda J. Child, *Boarding School Seasons: American Indian Families, 1900–1940* (1999). An excellent work of fiction that features two Cree protagonists and gives some sense of the Cree worldview is Joseph Boyden, *Three Day Road* (2005).

The histories of indigenous Northwest Coast peoples include Robert Boyd, *The Coming of the Spirit of Pestilence: Introduced Infectious Diseases and Population Decline Among Northwest Coast Indians, 1774–1874* (1999). Indigenous activism is addressed in a number of volumes, including Alexandra Harmon, *Indians in the Making: Ethnic Relations and Indian Identities Around Puget Sound* (1998). Local court records, mobility patterns, and methods for conflict resolution are analyzed in Brad Asher, *Beyond the Reservation: Indians, Settlers, and the Law in Washington Territory, 1853–1889* (1999); a consideration of the ways that methods of conflict resolution differ among a group of ethnically similar communities may be found in Bruce G. Miller, *The Problem of Justice: Tradition and Law in the Coast Salish World* (2001); and treaty making, the legal system, and regional economics are discussed in Roberta Ulrich, *Empty Nets: Indians, Dams, and the Columbia River*, 2nd ed. (2007). A classic by anthropologist Ruth Benedict, *Patterns of Culture* (1934) was reissued in 2005. See also Harry F. Wolcott, *A Kwakiutl Village and School* (2003); and Martine Jeanne Reid (ed.), *Paddling to Where I Stand: Agnes Alfred, Qwiqwasutinuxw Noblewoman* (2004).

Index

A

Alaska, 22, 23
  classification of ethnic groups, 26–27
  colonization of, 14–19, 67
  contemporary developments, 15–16, 18–20
  language, 21–22
  Norton culture, 7–9
  Paleo-Arctic traditions, 2–5
  Small Tool traditions, 6, 7
  Subarctic peoples of, 39–56, 63–76
  Thule culture, 9
Alaska Native Claims Settlement Act, 56, 101
alcohol, introduction and abuse of, 17, 18
Aleutian Islands, 4, 5–6, 14, 22, 26, 27
Aleut International Association, 20
Aleut language, 21, 22, 27
Aleuts, 1, 15, 20, 21, 26–27, 36–38, 95, 113
Algonquian-language speakers, 41, 53, 57–63
Alsea language, 78
American Arctic peoples, 1–20, 21–38
  classification of ethnic groups, 24–27

clothing of, 26
colonization and contemporary developments, 11–20
history of settlement, 1–11
linguistic makeup, 21–22
traditional cultures, 27–38
American Subarctic peoples, 39–56, 57–76
  assimilation policies and, 54
  contemporary developments, 54–56, 64, 69, 71
  cultural stability and adjustment, 54–56
  Eastern Subarctic zone, 41, 57–63
  enculturation of the young, 50–51
  ideology, 41–42
  material culture 44-46
  ownership and social organization, 47
  relationships among family and kin, 47–50
  settlement and shelter, 43–44
  spiritual convictions/ religion, 51–54, 59, 61, 62–63, 65, 67–68, 70, 71, 73, 75, 76
  territorial arrangement, 42–43
  Western Subarctic zone, 41, 63–76